YOUNG & SAVED

LIVING IN A WORLD THAT'S NOT LIKE YOU

DANE FRAGGER

Young and Saved: Living In A World That's Not Like You
By Dane Fragger

TABLE OF CONTENTS

INTRODUCTION

I was told that my young days were supposed to be the prime years of life. At least, this is what generation after generation tells you growing up. I believed the hype, and when I got to college, I was expecting the wildest days of my life. I thought life was going to be like it was in all the movies that I watched while growing up. I was planning on meeting new girls, going to new parties, and doing my own thing. However, just like Christian hip-hop artist, Trip Lee said, "God showed me a new picture of the good life." Suddenly, I went from meeting new girls to reading new Scriptures; and from going to parties to church revivals.

This was now my new fun, but after a while, it began to get harder. I started noticing that I was living this life differently than 99% of my peers. People began to avoid me because they would see my Jesus posts on Facebook. I started feeling like an outcast and that I was a part of a different world. The world used to love me and accept me, but it didn't anymore. As young believers, we start feeling like Lebron James when he left Cleveland to go to Miami. Everyone hated him. Cleveland fans despised him and burned his jerseys on barbeque grills. But when he came back, four years later, they all loved him again. This is how it feels to be young and saved. The world wants you back so that they can love you again, but you know that you can't go back.

Throughout this process of sticking with Jesus, you are challenged because you have no room to make any mistakes. The people that you left behind are now watching you. The cameras are always on you because everybody knows that you're a "Christian," so you can't mess up. Then when you do mess up, you're labeled as a hypocrite. Now you have the whole world calling you hypocritical, unloving, and judgmental. Being young, these challenges can cause you to feel alone in this world. Quite often you are the only saved person in the crowd. So, how are you to live in a world that's not like you?

This book will help answer that question and the others that you may have been too afraid to ask. It covers some of the most critical topics that young believers face, but in an honest, real, and biblical manner. This includes sex, dating, clubbing, smoking weed, drinking and many more topics. However, I wanted to make this book different. These themes are covered in a non-sugar-coated manner, and you will also learn of my downfalls. So, buckle up and fasten your seatbelts!

I pray that this book helps you grow and go further in Christ. I pray that it helps you keep the fire burning on the inside. At times, your fire may dwindle, but I pray this book will be the lighter fluid to your soul! In Jesus name, let every single chapter bless your soul.

Enjoy!

"Chug it! Chug it! Chug it!" is all I could hear, as I took big gulps of watermelon vodka that burned my throat and stomach.

I remember seeing girls go into bedrooms, bathrooms, and locker rooms, just to please a man or "two" because they longed for acceptance.

The things we do for acceptance...

CHAPTER 1
SOCIALLY AWKWARD

Longing For Acceptance

Have you ever been in a situation where someone makes a joke, and everyone in the room is dying of laughter except you? And in your mind, you're debating if you should just be nice and laugh along or keep your unchanging, non-laughing, stale face on. It's those awkward and uncomfortable moments that we hate the most. Recently, I was at a wedding, and someone made a sex joke about pornhub, and all of the groomsmen were laughing but me. Now if I weren't saved I probably would have laughed too. However, just to be nice, I did "think" about giving a little chuckle. My wife has always told me that I'm great at fake laughing. I've done it several times while listening to boring stories (not from her of course). But at this moment, fake laughing didn't feel right. I wanted to be accepted but just not that bad. So instead, I just put my head down, scrolled through my Instagram and acted like I wasn't paying attention. As the only one not laughing, I felt like an outcast, socially awkward, and different.

As young believers, these situations are quite common. Feeling socially awkward isn't unusual. So what are we to do? First, let's look at what it means to be socially awkward. Social awkwardness can be defined as "active but odd."[1] Active, because you're present, but **odd** because you don't fit in. Meaning, you are surrounded by people, but you just don't fit in. If we're honest, sometimes we just want to fit in, because it feels awkward standing out.

Do you remember growing up and seeing those kids that everyone laughed at because they were different? That's how it feels being a millennial Christian. We're the different one now; because we hold a different set of values than the vast majority of our peers. And it is easy to become discouraged when you're the only Christian at your school, job, or in your family. Additionally, it becomes even more awkward the moment people begin to realize that there is a difference between you and them. Have you ever had a conversation with someone and once they find out that you're a Christian, they change their whole demeanor towards you? They give you the **"Oh, okay, you're a Christian?"** Then you begin to hear the shocked tone in their voice. They're suddenly struck with this awkward feeling because now they don't feel as comfortable saying certain things around you. Sometimes they'll even stop cussing and try to be on their best behavior around you because they're afraid that you'll judge them. But you just want them to know that you're not out to condemn them and that you're just having a simple conversation. Now since they no longer feel comfortable around you, they'll either want to change you or avoid you, because you're not like them. We find ourselves in these situations often. However, as young believers, we must learn to be comfortable in them because being socially awkward is normal when you're saved.

Acceptance & Rejection

At times, it's difficult being socially awkward, because you'd rather be accepted than rejected. Acceptance is something that people long for. Most people want some level of acceptance by others. If you struggle with the need for acceptance, you will have a hard time being saved. Most people will not accept you; they will actually reject you.

The hard truth is that we will not be invited everywhere, nor will people always associate with us because we're different. You may have found yourself in a situation where every co-worker gets an invite to a birthday party or happy-hour, but you. Maybe you weren't planning on going, but you thought that they would at least ask you, right? And when they don't invite you, the rejection stings even more. WHATEVER YOU DO – please don't be the person that invites yourself because you weren't invited. You are better than that! I remember being that person once!

I was eight years old, and some kid in my class was having a huge party at a jungle gym. I was not invited, but I ended up finding out about it. I remember telling my dad about the party and how I was going to call my friend and figure out what time the party started. When I got home that night, I called my friend and said, "Hey what time is the party?" After finding out the time, I went and told my dad about the party, and he gave me the cold hard truth. He said, "Hey bud, I don't think that you were invited to that party." When my dad told me this, it finally hit me, I WASN'T INVITED. I then remember feeling embarrassed because I wanted to go to this party and be around this group of kids that didn't even want me there. I didn't fully realize all of this at the time, but I now see the rejection that I felt. That same rejection I felt at eight years old is how us, as believers, sometimes feel. But we must know that this type of rejection is normal, and we must get used to it. We are the rejects, and it's a part of the call.

Don't let this rejection bother you. It's better to be rejected by everyone and accepted by Jesus. It may sound cliché, but the only validation you need comes from up above, and that's Jesus. Although the world rejects you, Jesus stands with you! Yes, you may not be invited everywhere, but heaven welcomes you!

"But I Just Want to Be Accepted"

When you long for acceptance, you find yourself making decisions that you later regret. I've made several poor decisions in my life because I felt pressured and I didn't want to be the only one not doing it, so I did it. That's because I wouldn't have been accepted if I didn't do it. I didn't want to be left alone as the outcast of the group. After all, who really likes being the outcast?

When I was sixteen years old, I went to a house party, and I was the outcast because I was the only one there who had never tried alcohol. I didn't live for Jesus then, but I still had some convictions and alcohol just wasn't my thing. However, that night, everyone at the party found out that I had never taken a shot of alcohol before. So, what did they do? They encouraged me to grab the bottle and chug. What did I do? I grabbed the bottle and took a couple gulps. And as I was drinking, I remember them yelling, "Chug It, Chug it, Chug It" (I didn't chug the bottle). After I stopped drinking that night, I felt stupid. I started wondering why did I drink it? It made no sense, and the watermelon vodka didn't even taste good; it just burned my throat and stomach. But at that moment, I wanted to be accepted rather than being socially awkward.

Looking back, I wish I had stuck with my gut instinct, instead of trying to be someone that I'm not. Funny thing is, I didn't even talk to most of the people ever again after high school. It's crazy that we make big-time decisions with people that we never end up communicating with again. Sadly, sometimes, we have consequences from those decisions all because of this longing for acceptance.

Take a moment and think about one decision you made in your life that you really regret; a decision you made because you wanted to be accepted. After thinking about it, you probably wish you could go back in time and undo it. More than likely, whomever you were trying to impress wasn't even worth it. What I am saying is that we get tied to bad decisions because we don't want to be left out.

The devil wants us thinking that there is a problem being left out and different from everyone else. Well, I have good news for you! You are not everyone else, and you're different because God called you to be different. So never give yourself over to something that's not like you. I understand the need to be accepted by your peers but don't bend and don't let people pull you down because you're different. You must be comfortable being different because being socially awkward and rejected is a part of the call.

Daniel, Shadrach, Meshach, Abednego – The Rejects

I can only imagine how awkward it must have been for Daniel, Shadrach, Meshach, and Abednego in the Bible. They were the only four people in Babylon that stood up for God, and they were rejected because of it. They must have really felt like outcasts. However, they still didn't bend. Daniel continued praying even when it wasn't allowed; the lion's den couldn't stop him. Shadrach, Meshach, and Abednego didn't bow even though they would be sent to the fiery furnace. I could imagine them hearing their peers say, "just bow," "don't pray," "why can't you be like everyone else?" Nevertheless, these four Hebrew boys refused to give in. Put yourself in their shoes for a minute. Imagine being the only person in your city that worshipped God. Imagine the looks that people would give you. Imagine how people would call you crazy. Imagine how you wouldn't be welcomed anywhere. You would be the outcast of the entire city. But despite all of those oppositions, these four Hebrew boys remained unshaken. And because of that, they were able to see a miracle from God. No matter the awkwardness or possible repercussions, they stayed true to themselves. The lack of acceptance wouldn't bend them or break them. God is calling us young believers to be faithful to him, even when we're rejected. Never become a slave to acceptance.

Misfits Don't Fit In

As long as you are a misfit, you will be socially awkward. That's because you are the piece to the world's puzzle that doesn't fit. You are the misfit. Have you ever tried to fit a piece from a puzzle into a different puzzle, just to see if it will fit? But that piece never ends up fitting because it was never meant for that puzzle? That's what it means to be a misfit. You are on a different puzzle than the world. You're on the kingdom puzzle, and that's where your piece will always fit. That's why as misfits it's hard to function in society. We weren't meant to fit in with everyone, and we will forever be rejected by this society.

You cannot fit into a place that's not designed for you. You were designed for God's work here on this earth. Just like the world didn't receive Jesus, nor will they receive you, because you are different, you are a misfit.

Rudolph Was Rejected

Think about Rudolph the Red-Nosed Reindeer (Arthur & Larry, 1964)[2]. He was laughed at because he was different. He didn't fit in with the other reindeer because he had a red nose and no one else did. Even Rudolph's family tried to disguise his red nose because they were ashamed of it and wanted him to be accepted. And Santa Clause who is supposed to be nice didn't even want Rudolph on his team. However, it was Rudolph's red shining nose that got them through the storm on Christmas Eve. You may not be accepted, but you are still the light! They may not want you, but they sure do need you!

What am I saying? You have a red nose; you are the Rudolph in this world. You will not fit in with everyone because you are designed and purposed to lead. Rudolph's differences became his greatest tool! By the end of the story, it was Rudolph and his red nose that saved Christmas. People will laugh at you for being different, but at the end of the day, they will still need you! It's okay being a socially awkward misfit that's not accepted. It doesn't change who God has called you to be. You are the light that will get people through this cold world.

The World Will Not Accept You

I believe that as young people we can rally together as socially awkward people serving the everlasting God. We are the people who don't care about what the outside world thinks of us. It's not easy to ignore what everyone says, but it is worth it. Isn't funny how the world views us as the awkward ones when they're living in a world that was created by our God – who they rejected? So who should be the awkward ones? Us or them? The one that we serve created this world. Everything on the earth belongs to the Lord. If it is the Lord's, then us as his heirs, have dominion over it. Do not worry about being socially awkward in a world that is owned by our Father. You are the hope for this world! And hope doesn't long for acceptance!

Remember this, *"You are the light of the world—like a city on a hilltop that cannot be hidden."* (Matthew 5:14 NLT) People will hate this light, but they will also run to it. We must know our place here on this earth. Imagine running for your life through a dark forest, and after several miles, you finally see a light at the top of the hill. Instantly you will gain hope and seek that light. The Jesus in YOU is that light at the top of the hill that brings hope to this cold world. Don't worry about being socially awkward; you were born for this.

CHAPTER 2
CHRISTIAN DATING

"First comes love,
Then comes marriage,
Then comes the baby in the baby carriage."
(Jump Rope Rhyme, Author Unknown)

I know we all remember this nursery rhyme. However, to get to "First comes love" you have to go through "Christian Dating." This is probably one of the hottest topics in the Christian world. Who doesn't want to know more about "Christian Dating?" The thought of getting to know someone, loving them, marrying them, and having kids is a beautiful thing. In this chapter, I'll be covering the proper ways to date someone as a Christian. However, we must first acknowledge that God has made us to be attracted to the opposite sex. Men are made to love a woman. Women are made to love a man. It's natural for us to desire true love but we must do it right and with the right person. I personally encourage you to find someone who is on fire for the Lord. It's also good to be attracted to them spiritually and physically. There is nothing wrong admiring a beautiful face. In Genesis, Jacob was madly in love with a woman by the name of Rachel. The Bible called Rachel *"...beautiful in form and appearance"* (Genesis 29:17 ESV). And Rachel must've been really "FINE" for Jacob to work 14 years for her. However, "Christian Dating" is more than looks and attraction!

The "Christian Dating" Rule

When it comes to dating, there are a few things that we must uphold. First, as believers, we should not date outside of the Lord. Yes, this will step on a few toes, but if that girl or guy that you've been pursuing isn't saved, leave them alone. There is only trouble in a relationship with someone who doesn't have God's spirit. A quick side-note as well, just because someone does have God's spirit, doesn't mean that they are the right one for you either! There are plenty of people in your church that God didn't call you to marry! Do not get tied into a relationship with someone else who is saved just because the church pressures you into dating them. The church loves to play matchmaker, but let God be your matchmaker. God will lead you to the right SAVED person. Scripture tells believers to marry in the Lord. (1 Corinthians 7:39) If you're called to marry in the Lord, then you're called to date in the Lord as well.

"Do not be yoked together with unbelievers. For what do righteousness and wickedness have in common? Or what fellowship can light have with darkness?" (2 Corinthians 6:14 NIV)

You may have heard, "Don't be unequally yoked" but what does that really mean? The yoke described in the Scripture above is a wooden beam that goes around the neck of two oxen, and it is used for hauling heavy loads forward. However, this only works when the two oxen are very similar in physical and mental attributes. If one ox is stronger, taller, and faster than the other one, they will not successfully haul the heavy load because they aren't compatible. So instead of going forward, they'll just go in circles. Now, this is the same for a believer yoked with an unbeliever. There will be no Godly success in the relationship, and it'll never move forward. Instead, it will just go in circles because the two aren't compatible. How can a relationship work without any compatibility? Therefore, believers must yoke themselves with someone who is saved. No kingdom work will get done when the yoke around you and your significant other is off balance. Saved and unsaved will not produce anything good. Being equally yoked spiritually is the first step. However, it's also good to be equally yoked in goals, aspirations, and overall character.

The next part of 2 Corinthians 6:14 says, *"Or what fellowship can light have with darkness?"* If your significant other doesn't have God's spirit, then they are in darkness. The Bible also says, *"...Now if any man have not the Spirit of Christ, he is none of his."* (Romans 8:9 KJV) So what would be the purpose of dating someone who isn't one of God's? How can light and darkness make a good relationship? You're literally on two different teams. One of you is winning souls to God's Kingdom, and the other is winning souls to Satan's Kingdom.

The Bible says, *"Can two walk together except they be agreed?"* (Amos 3:3 KJV) How can you walk in the same direction with someone who has a completely opposite spiritual lifestyle than you? You serve the living God, and they don't. If the person is opposed to things of God, it's never going to work. On Friday nights, you'll want to go to the church revival or conference, and they may want to go to Coachella or some club. These are the reasons why you should date and marry in the Lord.

Boundaries

A healthy Christian relationship has boundaries. I believe that setting up boundaries is one of the most important things when it comes to dating. If there are no limits in place, your relationship will suffer. Boundaries are set so that no one crosses that forbidden line. Boundaries are not a bad thing; just make sure that they're healthy and realistic. Without them, there would be a lot more people falling into sin. Parameters help keep you from doing things that you shouldn't do. Forgive me for using an animal as an example when it comes to dating, but quite often, pet owners put up boundaries in their house so that their pets don't cross them. The reason for this is simple; there are some places that pets are not supposed to get into. In comparison, there are some things that believers in relationships aren't meant to get into either. Another example would be parents who place safety knobs on their oven. They are put in place so that the child does not start a fire. Without boundaries in a relationship, there will be a lot of wildfires burning.

"Can a man take fire in his bosom, and his clothes not be burned?" (Proverbs 6:26 KJV)

There are some things that you cannot expose yourself to, or you will get burnt. This is the reason why boundaries are healthy. Examples of healthy boundaries include:

There is no need to have your boyfriend or girlfriend over at your house alone

This boundary is set up because when you're alone with them, all of your sexual hormones flare up. Being alone with them usually leads to something else. When you're alone with them in your house, you'll be tempted to cuddle up on that bed, and once you are there, it's hard to stop. Also, when you're alone, you tend to dress a little less. Sometimes women will go braless and wear booty shorts around the house with their boyfriend. Men will go shirtless or walk around in boxers. I know these things by experience.

When alone, you are tempted on a whole different level because now there is no one around to keep you accountable. When there is no accountability around, sneaking in a quick sin doesn't sound like a bad idea; because "no one" will find out. Thoughts will run through your head like "I'll do it, just this one time and repent after." Next thing you know, you find yourself showering with your significant other and deeply involved in sin. This eventually becomes a habit. It's best to not put yourself in a position that will cause you to fall. It's better to be safe than sorry and repenting for your sexual sin.

Maintain your personal space

You aren't married yet. It is important that you still have a life. Your life cannot be consumed by the person you're dating. Am I telling you to stop hanging out with them a lot? No, not at all, keep spending time with them. If you're in a relationship right now, please don't use this section as a reason to stop hanging around your significant other. What I am saying though, is that personal space allows you to achieve things for yourself. I've seen some people in relationships sacrifice their entire life for someone that never committed to them in marriage. And when that person breaks up with them, they are left with nothing.

Recently, I read an interesting article on Stanton Peele's website titled, **"I gave up everything for my boyfriend and now that's he left, I'm desolate."** [3] In this post, the woman mentions how she became addicted to her boyfriend and threw away her entire life. Then once they broke up, she was devastated, she felt sick all the time and couldn't enjoy life. Let me tell you something; I don't care how good your relationship might be right now, YOU ARE STILL REPLACEABLE. I don't say that to instill fear in you, but you must maintain your own goals and personal space, especially while dating.

I don't mean you should be entirely independent until you get married, but there must be a balance. Enjoy some things for your-self because the person you are with right now may not be the one you marry. What a shame it would be to give up all your friends, hobbies, and yourself to someone that you don't even marry. We've all had that one friend that gets a boyfriend or girlfriend, and then suddenly they forget about their friends, family, and goals. When you maintain your "personal space," you can still keep close with your friends, family, and goals. If you're in a relationship where you cannot associate with your friends and relatives–you need to reevaluate that relationship because it's controlling. There's a big red warning flag above your relationship if your significant other doesn't allow you to have personal space. Just remember to keep yourself before giving yourself over in marriage. On the day when you both say "I Do," they can have all of you.

Get to Know the Person You're Dating

Through the entire dating process, it is crucial that you get to know them. I know it's easy to be in love and in a blissful utopian state, but you must know their ins and outs. I cannot stress this to you enough. The reason there are so many young divorcees is that people didn't learn enough about their spouse before getting mar-ried. And over the course of time, they changed, and true colors came out. Quite often you'll hear a spouse say, "I never knew they were like that until we got married." This is a statement you do not want to have to use in the future. When you come into a dating relationship with someone, make sure you know who they really are. It's important to know everything about them before you marry them. You need to know about their past, their likes and dis-likes, their future goals and where they want to live. You especially need to know how they like to use their money. The list is never-ending. Find out as much as you can about your significant other before you even get engaged to them.

Not only do you need to find these things out but you also need to observe your significant other in every season of their life. If you've only seen the happy side of them before going into a marriage, that's not good. You may not like the sad, depressed, and angry side of them that is eagerly waiting to be exposed. When someone is sad or angry, they can become a completely different person. When I am sad, I'm not the same Dane. I tend to keep quiet and not say much. If you can't handle your significant other in a season of sadness, it will not work. That's why it's good to see their sad, depressed, and angry sides. Once you see these sides, you'll know if you can handle it down the line when you're married.

Make sure that you play your part too and are vulnerable as well. Don't hide your emotions from your girlfriend or boyfriend, because one day the real you will leak out; and if they don't like that person, they will run. The key to a successful relationship is to be who you really are at all times. Don't hide the real you. When two people come together and are "real" with each other from day one, the chances of a successful relationship are much higher.

Additionally, in the process of getting to know them, it's important that you see them without all the makeup, nice haircuts, and fancy clothes. I don't mean that you should have a sleep-over to discover these things. Go on a date with each other and leave the makeup, nice haircut, fancy clothes, and fake hair at home. Your future spouse needs to know what you look like behind all of the decorations. A Christmas tree looks lovely when it is decorated, but remove those decorations, and it's just a plain tree. And there is nothing very appealing to look at. When you're married to someone, you will wake up to them without of all of the decorations. Can you handle how they look without the decorations? What if it's just too much for you? Fortunately, my wife and I are attracted to each other no matter how we look in the morning, but this isn't the case for every marriage. Some people struggle with seeing their spouse un-pampered. If that is you, remember that your love for your spouse should transcend looks. Additionally, if your spouse is not attracted to you in your worst looking state, there is a problem. They should still call you beautiful or handsome, even when you think that you look horrible.

How Saved Are They?

Getting to know your significant other is more than just learning their attitude, emotions, and character. You should also determine their level of "saved-ness." There are people in the church who were born again, that no longer enjoy the things of God. It would be awful to marry someone who you "thought" was saved. Just because they speak in tongues and raise their hands during worship doesn't mean that they have a real relationship with God. It's important to ask your significant other some questions so that you can see where their mind is spiritually. Along with that, find out what their desire for God is like. Will they be excited to go to church with you or is a couple church services a month enough for them? Will you be the only one on fire for the Lord or will they be on fire with you? Will they support you in ministry? Will they help you in ministry? I can't tell you how many couples I've seen where one is on fire for the Lord and the other is not. If the church is the biggest part of your life, then it's essential that you have the full support of your significant other or they may slow you down!

Also, make sure that you observe whether they get along well with others in your church. Be careful getting into a relationship with someone who has a problem with everyone in the church. People will always connect you to your significant other. If they're not getting along with anyone, it'll block opportunities for you. Not only will it prevent opportunities but people will not want to be around you because of them. The last thing you want is a drama-filled boyfriend or girlfriend. Avoid them it at all costs, and you will be happier in life.

God-Centered Relationship

Lastly, the most important thing in dating is to have a God-centered relationship. In a Christian relationship, your goal should be to grow in God together. There is a lot of power in a Christian couple that loves God "together." Don't let life keep you and your significant other from keeping God number one. I know you may work full-time, have school full-time, and have ministry duties, etc., but you must still find time to pray and read the Bible with your boyfriend or girlfriend. It may sound old school and traditional, but a lot of couples fail because they have removed God from the center.

When my wife and I first started dating, we would read the Bible together all the time. This might sound funny, but we would also pray in the spirit together on the phone as well. I believe that this spiritual connection helped us get through some attacks at the beginning of our relationship. But over time, we slowly stopped praying and reading the Bible together. We no longer allowed God to be the center and our relationship took some hard hits. Our relationship failed during that time. Eventually, we started talking again; we realized where we went wrong. We had neglected to keep God number one. We realized that we couldn't have a successful relationship without Jesus in it. Today, we are happily married, and God is once again number one.

In your relationship, there will be many spiritual, financial, and physical attacks. Your relationship will not stand through these battles if God is not at the center. A God-centered relationship can make it through anything. When God is the captain of your relationship, he can navigate it through the storms of life. Don't try to be the captain of your relationship, let God.

CHAPTER 3
CHRISTIAN SEX ED

What God Has to Say About Sex

Whenever you talk about sex, the room usually fills up with hidden smiles and low giggles. There's something about sex that fascinates the mind and brings curiosity to the body. However, it is essential that as young believers, we discuss this topic, in a real and biblical manner. You don't need another sugar-coated message on sex; you need a real one. Society will tell you all about sex, but they will not tell you the "God" honest truth. In the world, sex is glamorized, prized, and sought after. Sex is viewed as an accomplishment. When a man loses his virginity, the world calls it manhood, and he's praised for it. If he sleeps with several women, it's not called ungodly but seen as GOALS. There is something wrong with the way sex is viewed, and it's because we live in a sex-crazed society. Therefore, it's important that as young believers we're aware and equipped to handle the sexual pressures the world throws at us. In this chapter, I'll be talking about sex as a whole; which includes sexual intercourse and any other form of sexual relations. Anything past kissing is what is being covered.

What Is Sex?

For a moment, let's go back to fifth-grade Sex Ed, and get a clear definition of sex. Sex is when two people, male and female, come together and use their reproductive organs for sexual gratification. In an article Teen Vogue states, "**The average age of virginity loss for American men is 16.9 years old, and the average age for American women is 17.2 years old."** [4] This means people engage in sex before their high school graduation, marriage, and adulthood.

What is it about sex that causes people to make this decision before marriage? Why give your body to someone who can't even put a ring on your finger and marry you? Why be so vulnerable with someone who cannot give you their last name? The answer is that people are curious about sex and to be brutally honest, it feels good. However, God intended sex to be only for the husband and wife; not the boyfriend and girlfriend. Nor the best friend that's close to you and definitely not the one-night stand or the friend with benefits, but only for the married couple.

What Does the Bible Say About Sex?

"...It is good for a man not to have sexual relations with a woman. But because of the temptation to sexual immorality, each man should have his own wife and each woman her own husband." (1 Corinthians 7:1-2 ESV) These verses let us know that any sexual relations outside of marriage is considered sexual immorality, which is a sin. Paul also tells us that sexual relations are only for the husband and wife, not anyone else. If someone is engaging in anything sexual outside of marriage, it's wrong. No, you cannot escape sexual sin by partaking only in foreplay either. Premarital foreplay is wrong, just like premarital sex is wrong. Some believe that if you don't have sex and just touch each other, then you're okay. But again, all sexual things are for the husband and wife. The Bible also shows us that the first people to ever have sex together were married, and that

was Adam and Eve, *"Adam made love to his wife Eve, and she became pregnant and gave birth to Cain…"* (Genesis 4:1 NIV) Please notice it says, *"he made love to his wife…"* It was not his girlfriend, side-chick, or a man. It was his wife, Eve.

God gave sex two purposes. The first was for procreation and to populate the earth. Secondly, sex is for the enjoyment of married couples. God made sex to be a good thing. However, Satan perverted the original intent of sex. Satan has been glorifying premarital sex, homosexual sex, and many other forms of sex. However, it is still vital that as young believers we stand for sexual purity despite what the culture has to say. The culture is speaking loud and clear, but so is God. The culture says, "do it with whoever and whenever." God is saying to be pure and wait until you're married. Sadly, this does not always happen, and when it doesn't, we're left with consequences.

Sex and the Impact on the Christian World

Unfortunately, this thing called sex has tremendously affected believers of all ages across the entire world since the beginning of time. You can probably count on both of your hands, the number of people you know in the church that fell to pre-marital sex or adultery. The struggle with sex is not an uncommon thing, and more people are battling with it than you know. There are a lot of hidden sexual struggles that unfortunately stay hidden. When these actions go unchecked and untamed, damage takes place. Sex has actually worked against mankind because it's been responsible for millions of broken marriages. According to OneNewsNow.com, "35% of Christian married men have cheated on their spouses in an extramarital affair." [5] If your church has 1,000 married men, that means it's possible that 350 of them are having sex with women outside of their marriage. That's an alarming statistic that needs to change.

Throughout the Bible, we also see many believers that struggled with sex. For example, King David (who will be discussed more in a later chapter), was *"A man after God's own heart"* (Acts 13:22) yet he still fell to adultery. This man of God had such an urge burning within him that he ignored all possible consequences. While on his roof one night, he saw a beautiful married woman, bathing. Her name was Bathsheba. David couldn't resist her beauty though, nor did he care that she was married. He just saw her body bathing in the moonlight and wanted to make love to her, so he did. Because of this decision, David had a lot of repercussions. It clearly shows us that if you don't keep your sex hormones in check, you'll find yourself in bed with a Bathsheba and not thinking twice about the consequences.

An unhealthy hunger and desire for sex will blind you to the fact that you're married, that you serve the living God, and that it's wrong outside of marriage. Sex will push you to a place where you forget everything because you're horny. It can have such a stronghold on you that you'll do anything to get it. Sex will tell you to leave all convictions and morals at the door and come in and enjoy yourself. Then after you've enjoyed yourself, you're left with shame and potential lifelong consequences. An uncontrolled sex drive will get you in trouble. Do not become a part of the statistics, stay sexually pure.

Sexual Purity

"It is God's will that you should be sanctified: that you should avoid sexual immorality; that each of you should learn to control your own body in a way that is holy and honorable." (1 Thessalonians 4:3-4 NIV)

It is essential that you remain pure so that you can remain close to God. There are a lot of dangers tied to sex outside of marriage. When you have sex with someone outside of marriage, you're literally giving a piece of yourself away. That's because inside of sex there's a lot of passion, love, and fantasy. And when you connect yourself sexually with someone who is not married to you, they take something from you.

When I was first got filled with the Holy Spirit, I had to deal with a lot of issues because I had a lot of premarital sex. Every woman that I had sex with took a piece of me. There was a period of time where I couldn't stop having vivid images and memories of my sexual encounters with different women. All day long, images would just pour into my mind like a Google download. When I finally started to get my life right, those memories kept getting a hold of me. I stand now delivered from that, but it was a consequence of having pre-marital sex. That is what sex does outside of a marriage covenant; it latches onto you and becomes hard to shake off.

When you have sexual encounters with someone, you'll probably have vivid dreams about the encounter for a while. It's a tool that Satan uses to bring God's children back under bondage. If you are currently dealing with the repercussions of your sexual past, I bind them and cast them out in the name of Jesus. This is very serious because it just takes one thought to bring you back to the sexual bondage. There is a lot of power in sex, and that's why it should only be done through marriage.

Many people have a hard time breaking up with someone who took their virginity. Sex outside of marriage creates an emotional tie that is extremely hard to break. That is why most people still "love" the person that took their virginity. Sex creates an undoable bond. There is nothing more emotional and vulnerable than having sex with someone. When you have sex with someone, you're exposing every part of you. You are removing the veil and exposing all of you. This type of vulnerability placed in the wrong hands is very dangerous, and the wrong hands are someone outside of marriage.

You were not meant to have sex with multiple people, only your spouse. When you rack up the numbers in the bedroom and finally get married, you may have some sexual troubles with your spouse. This is because you set a certain expectation in the bedroom that was never supposed to be set outside of marriage. When you get married, you may start comparing your spouse to your former sexual partners. Sex with your spouse may not seem as good because you're comparing it to your previous sexual encounters and fantasies. Eventually, your comparisons will turn into ungodly wants, and you will soon desire sex outside of your marriage. Some people have a form of respect for their spouse, so instead of having sex with someone else; they have sex with themselves through pornography or mental screenshots of their former sex partners. We are now beginning to see that ungodly sex leads to more issues. This is another reason why you need to live sexually pure. I know it is not always easy to remain pure because sometimes you do burn with passion, but if you're not married, you must control yourself. Even if you are married, you still need to control of yourself because there is temptation around every corner.

Sexual Purity in Relationships

For those that are saved and in a relationship, I know the sexual temptation is there. It's hard not to be sexually attracted to someone that you're dating. Because of this attraction, many have crossed the sexual line. Some will keep crossing it, and some are fighting to stay pure. If you're currently not pure, it's important to bring those boundaries back before you run into more trouble. Sexual impurity delays the blessings of God on your life and in your relationship. Unmarried sex creates a wedge between you and your significant other, and between you and God. God cannot be the center of a relationship when fornication is involved. Sin will always separate, divide, and destroy.

Prior to dating and marrying my wife, sex was one of my struggles. Unfortunately, I brought some of those habits into our relationship. Throughout the course of our dating, we had struggled with sexual purity. Fornication was not a common thing in our relationship, but there were times that we slipped up when God was looking for our purity, not our half-stepping. Because of our lack of self-control, we ran into a lot more problems.

If you are in a relationship or looking to have one down the line; leave all sexual relations at the door so that you can walk in the abundance of God's blessing. The best advice I can give you regarding sexual purity is to set real boundaries because it wants to creep into your relationship. For those stuck in sexual impurity; kick it out before it continues to do more damage. Sexual immorality is like cockroaches in a dirty house. Many more will come, and it will get harder and harder to keep the house clean. Plus, it's important to care for the soul of your significant other.

Show that you care by remaining pure and putting boundaries up. I know you want them to be attracted to you but don't tempt the person God has placed in your life. On your nightly FaceTime calls, keep covered up and genuinely care for their soul. Some things just shouldn't be seen until the words "I Do" are said. Real love means staying sexually pure until marriage because you care about where your significant other will spend eternity.

Freedom from Sexual Strongholds

Lastly, I want to discuss how you can be free from your sexual strongholds. First, remember, you will never be free while you keep doors opened. A good sign that you're not ready to be free is that you have not closed "every" door. Ungodly sex is a door that many believers don't want to shut until they get married. However, you cannot trick God, nor can you beat the system. Lust doesn't go away just because you get married. You must shut all doors now and actually win this battle. To be free, you must be honest with yourself and acknowledge the fact that there is a struggle. It is nothing to be embarrassed about; many people are bound by sex. If you desire to be free, all you have to do is call upon Jesus and ask him to deliver you from those sexual impurities.

You may get delivered (set completely free) quickly, or your deliverance may be a process. However, no matter the state of your deliverance, keep all doors shut and delete everything. You cannot be set free from sexual sin when you still have naked pictures on your phone or when you're still friends with that guy or girl on Snapchat that sends you dirty pictures every night just before you go to bed. If you're reading this now and you have things that you need to delete, just do it now because it's worth it. I know you may be debating with yourself about deleting the pictures because you'll never get them back, but trust me you don't need them back. I used to hate deleting naked pictures until I realized it felt better to be free. Plus, you are called, and you are worth much more than whatever is holding you back. Don't be afraid to be free; I promise God will deliver you if you're serious about it. The main reason some people never get freed is that they're not ready to leave. Some people rather sit chained up with the key right next to them, instead of experiencing God's freedom. God isn't going to forcefully take something from you that you're holding onto so tightly.

When you do get completely delivered, it is very important that you never to allow it back in again. Don't be like the cigarette smoker who stops for a week and goes right back to it. Stay delivered. I want to encourage you that you're not alone in your struggle and even when you feel the most vulnerable to fall into sexual sin, the Lord's strength will be your weapon. Next time when you're weak and on the edge of giving in, allow God to give you strength. His strength will come in different ways. Sometimes he'll put a Scripture in your head, or someone close to you may call. Whatever way of escape God provides, just follow it. God really does love you. Give God your yes and sexual sin your no.

"My grace is sufficient for thee: for my strength is made perfect in weak-ness." (2 Corinthians 12:9 KJV)

CHAPTER 4
WHAT'S ACCEPTABLE?

The Can and Cant's of Christianity

"What can I do as a Christian without sinning?" is the question that many ask. But unfortunately, this question often goes left unanswered, or it's given a poor response. Many Christians will respond to controversial questions with, "No you can't do that because it's wrong." If you ask, "Why is it wrong?" the response will be, "Because Christians can't do that." Those days are over, and it's time that you get biblical answers for controversial questions. In this chapter, I will be covering clubbing, dancing, drinking, and smoking weed!

Our Image

Before identifying what's acceptable, we must first identify who we are. When we know who we are, we can better understand, why we don't do certain things. *"We are therefore Christ's ambassadors..."* (2 Cor 5:20 NIV) As ambassadors, we are the representatives of Jesus Christ on this earth, and we must talk, walk, and live like it. When you were growing up, your parents may have told you that you represent them, so be on your best behavior. And if you weren't, you would be in trouble. My parents told me this often, and I now see why. It's because your child represents you at all times. Your child has your last name; they are your seed and your reflection. And if the child gets in trouble, guess who gets the call? The parent.

In the same manner that a child represents their parent, a believer represents God. A child of God carries the name of Jesus, they are his seed, and his reflection. So if us as children of God represent God, than we cannot act in a way that does not adequately represent Him. Everywhere we walk, we are holding a banner high that says Jesus. With that being said, we believers are supposed to be the spitting image of Jesus in our words and actions. We cannot represent holiness and live unholy at the same time. Our actions must always match who Jesus is. However, sometimes this doesn't happen because we participate in things contrary to the way that God expects us to live. This is the reason why we need to know what is acceptable.

Dances and Clubs

I once saw an image spreading across social media that I will never forget. On one side of the picture, there was a man dancing "grinding" on a woman on the dance floor. On the other side of the picture, that same man was holding his hands up and worshipping God. The picture said Saturday night vs. Sunday morning. After seeing that picture, I thought to myself "Man, we have to be better because this is how the world sees us."

The outsiders of Christianity view is in this hypocritical manner. They believe that we're just all talk. The person that I saw sharing this photo was laughing and making a joke out of it because it was true. I could not deny the picture either because I knew people that club on Saturday and worship on Sunday. I know that if I wasn't a believer and I saw someone who claimed to be a Christian, dancing and grinding on a woman, I would be laughing and calling him or her a hypocrite too. This is what non-believers are doing to believers; they're laughing at us because we've modeled Jesus poorly at times. There is an image of what a Christian should look like here on this earth. That image doesn't include being at clubs or dances because of the things that take place there.

If you've ever been to a club or dance before, you know that nothing Godly happens there. Yes, even Prom and Homecoming, which we love so much, there's nothing but sin on the dance floor. When you think about these types of dances it's usually a room full of people grinding on one another; then switching to someone else and doing the same thing. I'm neither a rocket scientist, nor a crazy theologian (yet), but it is no secret that God doesn't want you dry humping with someone unless you're married to them.

Imagine if you suddenly lost your life while rubbing up on someone, or better yet, if Jesus were to come back tonight for his people, would you want to be caught doing that? Lol, I highly doubt it. Interestingly, dancing is one of the closest things to sex but with your clothes on and it's also one of the most accepted things across the world. It is sad that society has normalized men and women dry humping each other to music. Instead of it being called sin, it's called fun. I know I sound like a parent right here, but it blows my mind that parents would be okay with what their children do at dances. I'm not a parent yet, but I couldn't imagine having a daughter and knowing that she was out there dancing on a man like he's her husband. Dirty dancing has indeed shown the real morals of our society.

Sometimes people believe that a dirty dance is merely innocent. If you believe that, ask yourself if you would you go to the back of your car with every single person you danced with and dry hump them? I highly doubt it. If you are willing to dance dirty with them, does it really matter if you take them to your back seat for some action? Essentially, you're doing the same thing, expect one setting is in a crowd of people and the other is just you two alone. By making this comparison, you can see how dirty dancing really isn't innocent at all. It's just a gateway to deeper sin; because it arouses your sexual hormones and gets you wanting more from that person. A lot of one-night stands started with a dance.

As a young believer, it's easy to get caught up in these clubs and dances. Most people tell themselves "it's a special night" or "I don't do it often. Therefore, it's okay." Or, "It's prom, it's once in a lifetime thing." My favorite is, "It's my best friends 21st birthday, I have to support them." You then tell yourself, "I'll just go, say hi, and leave" but it never ends up that way. Once you get there, your friend will drag you to the dance floor; you'll have a couple drinks and boom; you're doing the very thing you said you weren't going to do.

Now tell me this, have you ever seen any form of purity on the dance floor when a song comes on about dropping it low and twerking? Probably not, because there is no purity when it comes to dancing in a sexual manner, with someone you're not married to. Am I saying that every form of dancing is sexual and wrong? No! However, there are forms of dancing that are sinful.

The Bible says, *"Now the works of the flesh are manifest, which are these; Adultery, fornication, uncleanness, **lasciviousness**,"* (Galatians 5:19 KJV) I want to focus on the tongue twister word "lasciviousness" (try saying it fast 3 times) and how it pertains to dirty dancing. J.H. Thayer defines lasciviousness as "Indecent bodily movements, unchaste handling of males and females, wanton (acts or) manners." [6] When you turn the music up and put all of those fancy words together, you get dirty dancing.

An article from Speaking Sound Doctrine has the following to say about lasciviousness and dirty dancing, *"Lasciviousness is appli-*

cable to any form of dance that, outside the bonds of marriage, would provoke lustful thoughts by bodily movements. This will include any dancing
that draws visual attention to those body parts pertaining to
sexuality. This condemns the typical popular fast dance that involves
swirling and gyrating the hips, buttocks, and pelvis and shaking the
breasts." [7]

I want to draw attention to the words "provoke lustful thoughts
by bodily movements" [8] because this is what dirty dancing does in
a nutshell. Dancing like this stirs you up and not in the right way.
Even though society has normalized this type of dancing, we as
believers cannot participate in this. Don't let the prom dresses and
fancy tuxedos fool you because sin is still taking place. As believers,
we must separate ourselves from participating in these social settings.

It is clear that dirty dancing is wrong, but some ask, "Can you
go to the club and just hang out if you're not dancing or drinking?"
The answer is no. The Bible says, *"Blessed is the one who does not walk
in step with the wicked or stand in the way that sinners take or sit in the
company of mockers."* (Psalm 1:1 NIV) After reading that, you must
ask yourself, how can you be blessed when you're surrounding
yourself with sin and coming into agreement with people engaging
in sinful behavior? In my eyes, that's not blessed because that's the
opposite of the scripture. We must face reality and understand that
some settings are just not for believers. And when our presence is
there, we're giving our stamp of approval.

Clubs and dancing are things that the world does, not the
church. The world is the system in place here on this earth that it
is opposed to the things of God. The devil is the one who has perverted society into thinking these things are okay. Let's not tie
ourselves to things of the world. It is hard because it seems as if
everyone else is doing it, but we must stay strong because purity is
free and sin cost. The next time your friend invites you to the club,
show them this chapter.

"Do not conform to the pattern of this world..." (Romans 12:2 NIV)

"...don't you know that friendship with the world means enmity against God? Therefore, anyone who chooses to be a friend of the world becomes an enemy of God." (James 4:4 NIV)

Alcohol and the "Casual Christian Drinker"

Drinking is another hot topic for millennial Christians. You may be the casual drinker or maybe you've just observed someone in your church post pictures of themselves drinking beer or taking shots of alcohol on their Instagram stories. Either way, this topic is interesting because many churches have different views on alcohol. Typically speaking, most churches forbid drinking because they know it can lead to getting drunk. It's not that every church believes that having a glass of wine will send you hell, but, they fear you will abuse it if they approve it. They believe that you may drink the entire bottle, rather than just a glass of wine.

Personally, I do not drink. The reason I do not drink is that I believe it can taint the image of Christ on me. My goal as a believer is to present myself without any excuses as to why someone can't receive my testimony. This doesn't neglect the fact that many will not receive you regardless of whether you drink or not, but it's good to be without excuse. Drinking is often associated with things that Christians don't do. If someone sees me out drinking, there's a chance I'll be labeled as a hypocrite and to be honest I don't need that extra label.

While being saved, there were times where I did have a glass of wine. I quickly stopped because I found myself having a glass of wine after stressful days. Some days when I got home, I started looking forward to that drink, and that wasn't how I wanted to live my life. I didn't want to be self-reliant on something so dangerous. I was never drunk, but I wanted to represent Jesus properly in my home and outside of my home. Is a small glass of wine is really worth the risk anyways? If you want something cold and fizzy, get some soda or even better get some sparkling cider (Trader Joes has the best), you don't really need alcohol.

What purpose does alcohol truly need to serve in the life of a believer? Do you drink it because you like the taste? Truthfully, alcohol, for the most part, does not taste good (especially hard liquor). The burn you feel as it goes down your throat is not a pleasant feeling. Or even better, does anyone actually like puking at the end of the night?

Alcohol is usually consumed with the hopes of getting intoxicated, or it's used to "relieve stress." When your friends drink, do you ever hear them say, "I'm just going to drink a little, I don't want to get drunk?" Probably not. When I used to go to parties, I don't remember hearing anyone say that. I remember everyone taking shots and trying to get wasted.

When you look in the Bible, you'll quickly find that getting drunk is a sin. There's not much debate in the Christian world that getting drunk is wrong because Scripture clearly states that it is.

"Nor thieves, nor covetous, nor drunkards, nor revilers, nor extortioners shall inherit the kingdom of God." (1 Corinthians 6:10 KJV)

I won't go out on a limb and say that a sip of wine is wrong, but I would not recommend drinking it either. When I see some of my Christian friends getting beers, it cautions me because I know that in the public's eye, they will not be viewed as people of the light. Christians who drink alcohol, especially in public, create stumbling blocks for believers and non-believers. Believers will question their salvation and nonbelievers will view them as hypocrites. Before I was saved, I once viewed a Christian man as a hypocrite because I saw him drinking a big glass of beer at a restaurant. It was right after church, and he was still in his church clothes, and he was less than a mile from the church. I remember being completely shocked and wondering if he was actually saved. Remember, I was not saved yet, and I had no room to talk because my sins were much worse than a glass of beer. However, it shows how unsaved people view Christians drinking.

The Bible teaches us that alcohol was consumed for many different reasons. At times, it was used to ease the stomach and other times for enjoyment. Still, the Bible does show you the consequences of alcohol. In Genesis 9:21, Noah got so drunk that his sons found him naked. In Genesis 19:34, Lot, who was a righteous man, drank so much wine that he slept with his own daughters. Too much alcohol will distort your mind, and it will cause you to make decisions that you will later regret. Imagine being Lot. Imagine waking up to realize that you slept with your own daughters. His huge mistake was birthed out of drinking alcohol. While it is clear that the Bible forbids getting drunk, as believers you should strive to steer away from alcohol altogether. It's not that having a sip of wine will send you to hell, but you don't want to taint the image of Christ on you or have an experience similar to Lot's.

Legalized Weed (Marijuana)

Another interesting topic among young believers is smoking weed. For many years people would say, "Weed is okay because it's an herb that God made." However, many Christians would argue with that statement by saying it's wrong because it is illegal and you must obey the laws of the land. Unfortunately, that response can no longer be used because weed is actually legal in some states and one day it may be legalized everywhere. So, is it okay to smoke weed? No. Smoking weed or using any other type of mind-altering drug is wrong.

The Bible says, "…be sober-minded." (1 Peter 5:8 ESV) Even if Peter's statement is referring to alcohol, it still shows you how God intends the state of our mind to be. God clearly desires that we have a sober mind. There should be no question about that. A sober mind is unimpaired, clear, and sensible. Anything that keeps you from being sober-minded would be contrary to Scripture whether it's alcohol, marijuana, or any other drug.

Weed also has some of the same side-effects as alcohol. Alcohol probably does have more of an impact on you, but weed can impact you as well. Both can be used to alter the state of your mind. Your reaction time is impaired when you drink alcohol or smoke weed. When your reaction time is slowed, you're unable to operate a motor vehicle properly. If your mind can be altered with weed, why smoke it?

I believe that God is calling us to have a sober mind and weed will not get us there. I'd be willing to bet that you have never seen someone high and sober-minded at the same time. It's not possible; it's an oxymoron. And just because the words, "weed," "marijuana," or "pot" are not mentioned in the Bible, it does not mean that God approves it. As believers, we should flee from weed because it's contrary to having a sober mind.

"Therefore, preparing your minds for action, and being sober-minded..." (1 Peter 1:13 ESV)

"...Therefore be self-controlled and sober-minded for the sake of your prayers." (1 Peter 4:7 ESV)

"Be sober-minded; be watchful..." (1 Peter 5:8 ESV)

The Other Effects of Weed

For the last several years, there have been many debates as to whether weed is an addictive substance. Many people who smoke weed believe that it's not an addictive drug. However, if weed isn't somewhat addictive, then why has it continued to destroy so many lives? If you look at collegiate and professional sports over the last few years, you will find that weed has been responsible for ruining many careers. Hundreds of collegiate athletes lose full-ride scholarships each year because they can't stop smoking weed. There are NFL athletes that would rather smoke weed than earn millions of dollars a year playing a sport that they love. An article from Addict-Help has this to say to about marijuana, *"Clinical studies, diagnostic and laboratory research, as well as anecdotal evidence, has shown that marijuana use can and does lead to dependence, abuse, and addiction. Marijuana over-stimulates the endocannabinoid system in the brain, leading to both psychological and physical dependency. In fact, nearly 10 percent of people who smoke marijuana will eventually develop a dependency."* [9]

One thing in this article really stood out to me: the words, "physical dependency." [10] I had several friends in high school that couldn't function without smoking weed. If they stopped smoking marijuana, even for a day, they would literally start throwing up. Without a puff of weed, they weren't content with life. Every moment of the day they were thinking about the next time they would get a chance to smoke. Some of my friends were so dependent on weed that they would even get high before playing football games. I have a hard time believing that pot is not addictive because I've seen the damage it has done to a lot of my friends. I watched good kids go completely downhill just from smoking weed. Fortunately for me, I never really latched onto it. I smoked it on a few occasions because I wanted to see what it felt like to get high, as so many people raved about it. However, each time I smoked it, I never got high. Maybe I smoked it wrong or maybe it God was keeping me. Nevertheless, I am grateful that I didn't experience it because I would've hated to be hooked on it like so many of my friends were. Whether weed is addictive or not, it has definitely damaged many lives.

Weed is also viewed as a gateway drug because drug abusers usually start by smoking weed. After weed, it's usually cocaine or ecstasy. Did you also know that sorcerers use marijuana and other forms of drugs as a part of their demonic rituals? Witches, sorcerers, and psychics use weed to channel demonic spirits and enhance demonic experiences. "Now the deeds of the flesh are evident, which are: immorality, impurity, sensuality, idolatry, **sorcery**..." (Galatians 5:19-20 NASB) Look at the word sorcery. A well-known Christian website, GotQuestions.org has this to say about drugs and sorcery:

"Interestingly, the New Testament Greek word translated "sorcery" is *pharmakeia*, which is the source of our English word *pharmacy*. In Paul's day, the word primarily meant "dealing in poison" or "drug use" and was applied to divination and spell-casting because sorcerers often used drugs along with their incantations and amulets to conjure occult power." [11]

Concluding Thoughts About Weed

Weed, or marijuana, has many different usages. But the primary use is to get high. As noted above, weed impairs your mind and God wants you to have a sober mind; not an impaired one. You cannot be high and right with God at the same time. The good news is that God can give you a high that you cannot even come close to experiencing with weed. Let's vow to keep our minds sober.

CHAPTER 5
MY TESTIMONY

From Past to Present

I couldn't write a book about being young and saved without giving you a little bit of my story. My story is still being written, but this is what I have so far.

Pre-Jesus

I grew up in the church from the womb, but I wasn't serious about getting close to God until I was 18. I remember being in church Sunday after Sunday, Wednesday after Wednesday, and not having a care in the world about living for God. Often during church, I would daydream about what I am going to do after church. I would think about what girl I was going to text, and who I was going to beat in video games later that day. I remember going to youth services and seeing people on fire for God. The only thing that got me excited about youth service was getting to dress down for church on a Sunday. I only enjoyed it because I got a chance to show off my LRG clothes. My mind was far away from Jesus. I believed in Jesus, I prayed over my food, and occasionally would pray on my own or even read the Bible, but a relationship with Jesus was just not a priority at that time.

The only things on my mind were football, girls, and music. If I had those three things, I was happy. However, I did have loving parents that would encourage me to keep God first and fully submit to him. Unfortunately, those good things my mom and stepdad told me about God, went in one ear and out of the other. I was blind to the things of God, heaven and hell were the last things on my mind. I was 16 years old and not thinking one bit about life after death. As I'm writing this now, I can really see how Satan had me distracted with the temporary things that were not right for me.

On the Edge

Growing up, I had some very uncomfortable stomach problems; yes, this is random, but it'll make sense soon. These stomach problems would make me very nauseous and anxious after every single meal. It was so bad that I literally carried a bottle of Pepto-Bismol around in my backpack in high school. Through this sickness, I actually started to understand that I needed the healing power of Jesus. Slowly, this now seventeen-year-old boy began to pray more often because I didn't want to be sick and I knew Jesus was a healer. This sickness was now opening a door of prayer in my life, and I slowly began to become more aware of the things of God. Then one day there was a shift in me, and I couldn't enjoy my sin as much. After I sinned, I would be hit with this irreversible guilt. I would feel wrong, dirty, and violated and this wasn't something I was used to. I remember telling a close friend of mine that I wasn't going to have sex with girls anymore because it was wrong. I had good intentions, but I was actually lying through my teeth. I wanted to stop fornicating so bad, but I couldn't control myself. I remember being afraid to go to bed, especially after sinning because I thought that I would wake up in hell. At night, after I got done sinning, I would often call my friend (at the time) who later became my wife. I did this because she was one of my only saved friends. I would talk to her on the phone until I fell asleep because I feared I was going to hell. I figured that maybe God would spare me from hell that night because I was on the phone with someone saved. But throughout this time, not much changed, I just kept sinning and feeling wrong afterward.

My senior year of high school was now ending, and I had a big two-day track meet ahead. I needed a good performance because the state meet was right around the corner. Fortunately, on the first day of the competition, I had the best performances of my entire life. Throughout the day I began to realize that it was the supernatural hand of God that was blessing me. I outdid my personal best in the long jump by three whole feet. It was crazy, and my mind was blown at how God literally made me fly. So that night when I got home, I did the unthinkable because I wanted God to bless me even more for day two. So, I took a big step towards God; I deleted every single naked picture on my phone. I did this to show God that I was "serious" about him, but truth be told, I really just wanted to be great again, at the track meet. I figured that God would bless me if I did a few things right.

So that's where my relationship with God stood, I wanted to be "friends with benefits." I wanted God's blessings, but I didn't want to submit my life to him fully. At that time, things really were not changing; I just continued in my sin. At times after I sinned, I would stand up, lift my hands up and ask God to fill me with his spirit. This was just a pattern for me because I couldn't shake the sin off. Nor could I wash it off, hot showers after sex couldn't give me the cleansing that I needed nor could it wash away the guilt that I felt. Deep down my soul was longing for God, but my flesh wanted sex.

The Decision

Throughout high school, I would often tell myself, "I will get saved at the age of 27." I just wanted to live "young, wild, and free" like Wiz Khalifa said. I wanted to do whatever my heart desired, and salvation wasn't on my mind at all. But what was so special about the age of 27? Why was 27 the perfect age to come to Jesus? I had believed that it was a good age for salvation because I could get all of the fun out of me. By the time I was 27, I had figured that the clubs would dry up and I would be done messing around with women, and I would finally settle down with one. I thought that this was the perfect plan but what I didn't know was that Jesus had an entirely different plan for me. I never expected to be writing a book about living saved before I was 27. Little did the 17-year-old Dane know, but salvation was a decision for right now; it wasn't tomorrow, it wasn't at 27, it was right then and there. So, at 17 salvation was staring me down and wouldn't look away.

Fast forward a little to the end of summer right before my freshman year of college. I was now eighteen years old, and I had just gotten back to my hometown from visiting my dad's house all summer. I was still sinning and "repenting" going into to my freshman year of college, but one day at church would change my life forever.

It was Sunday, September 25, 2011. Our church had a guest speaker that morning to preach. Now even though I wasn't living right, I still served as an armor-bearer in my church. Every Sunday morning, I would assist my pastor before, during, and after service. This armor-bearer position required me to sit in the very front row of the church. On this particular Sunday, I just knew without a shadow of a doubt that God's spirit was going to move in the church. I deliberately sat back a few rows, so I could avoid an encounter with God. I didn't want to get caught in the crossfire of God's spirit because I was embarrassed that I didn't already have His spirit. How stupid it was for me to avoid the very thing I was longing for. It's crazy how Satan puts fear in you to keep you from God's promises. As the service continued, I could feel the living God's presence on me. Then the time of service came where, if you're not living for Jesus, most people feel awkward, this part of the service was the altar call. I remember knowing that I needed to go down and give my life fully to Jesus. But at that moment, my heart was beating out of my chest; I begin to get nervous, as tons of people were making their way to the altar. All these people went down, but me.

Then as the altar call was starting to conclude, something crazy happened. I heard my name "Dane" called. It was so loud that I began turning around to figure out who just called my name during altar call?

A couple minutes go by that seemed like forever because, in my head, I was fighting between life and death. What do I do? I then began to realize whose voice it was that called my name. It was Jesus' voice. So, I made THE DECISION to go down and give my life to Jesus. I snuck back to the altar call room because I was still embarrassed. As I walked into the room, the guest speaker tells me, "He is ready for you professor." At that moment, I knew I was making the right decision. I had finally made the decision to give God all of me. I prayed in the altar call room to receive the baptism of the Holy Ghost, which is God's Spirit that infills us. I didn't receive it that day, but one of my pastors told me to come back on Wednesday night and that God was going to fill me with his Spirit.

When I got home from church that Sunday evening, I remembered a prophetic word that was spoken over me and recorded on a tape a couple years ago in high school. I knew that the tape was somewhere in the garage. However, I hadn't seen the tape in years, and I didn't even remember what was said on the tape. I went to the garage to look for the tape, and I saw my old clear container box with all my junk in it. I saw the tape with my name on it, labeled Dane 06-07-08. I slid my hand in and grabbed it. I went upstairs and asked my mom for a tape player. I got the tape player and sat down and listened to it. On the tape, the prophet told me, **"I see a decision that you're going to have to make in 2-3 years about whether it's the counsel of the Lord you will seek."** He was saying that in 2-3 years I'm going to have to make a decision to live for the Lord. When I heard those words, my mind was blown because it was 3 years later just like the prophet had said. In those 2-3 years, not once did I think about the tape nor did I remember any word about having to make a decision. God is so real that he gave a man who didn't know me a special word about a future decision that I was going to make. That Sunday evening, I was in complete awe about what God spoke.

Three days later, I went back to church for the Wednesday night service. I went back to the prayer room and received God's Spirit with the evidence of speaking in tongues. I spoke in tongues as they did in the Scripture that was written over 2,000 years ago. I was so excited because I had finally received God's Spirit and I was one of his!

"All of them were filled with the Holy Spirit and began to speak in other tongues as the Spirit enabled them." (Acts 2:4 NIV)

"While Peter was still speaking these words, the Holy Spirit came on all who heard the message. The circumcised believers who had come with Peter were astonished that the gift of the Holy Spirit had been poured out even on Gentiles. For they heard them speaking in tongues and prais-ing God. Then Peter said, 'Surely no one can stand in the way of their being baptized with water. They have received the Holy Spirit just as we have.' So he ordered that they be baptized in the name of Jesus Christ..." (Acts 10:44-48 NIV)

Battles

After receiving God's spirit on September 28, 2011, I was filled with joy. But the next couple days were awful. For the longest time,

I had pictured that once I got saved, everything would be easy and that I wouldn't have too many concerns.

But that day, I learned why a lot of church people say that the devil is a liar. I experienced it firsthand. All day, I kept having these crazy thoughts. The thoughts would be "God is not real," "You're not saved," "You're not really speaking in tongues." These thoughts were like a broken record in my mind, and they just wouldn't stop. They continued day and night. The only time I had peace of mind was in my sleep.

I would constantly ask God for forgiveness, all day because I felt wrong for having these thoughts. I was asking for forgiveness so much that my face would hurt from praying all day. The thoughts in my mind were increasingly getting worse, and I began having re-runs of all my sexual encounters. The images were so vivid, and I couldn't shake them loose. It was awful. These thoughts were ruining my life. I felt so ashamed.

Maintaining

Fast-forward to about a year later; I found myself having an even a harder time fighting these battles. They continued to weigh me down to point where I wasn't even myself anymore. I became a very awkward person at times because my mind was under this demonic chain. The thoughts became so evil; that I wouldn't even dare write them in this book. There were times that I would come home after school and just stay in my room all day because I had no peace. I felt lost, and I didn't know what to do. I felt like I was sitting in a dark room with no hope. I honestly didn't want to live anymore. It was so bad that some nights when I was driving on the freeway, I would just hope that I would get into a crash and die; because it would be better than dealing with these thoughts. There even came the point when I stopped reading the Bible and praying because I was just tired and worn out from these spiritual attacks.

Then one night when I got home from class, I went straight to my room and turned off all of the lights. I sat alone in this dark room, full of misery. I finally decided to crack open the Bible again and catch up where I last left off. I went to my Bible reading plan, which was several days behind, and started reading.

"You are the salt of the earth; but if the salt loses its flavor, how shall it be seasoned? It is then good for nothing but to be thrown out and trampled underfoot by men." (Matthew 5:13 NKJV)

I was shocked when I saw that this verse was included in my reading plan because earlier that day I came across Matthew 5:13 from a daily Bible verse app. Then within five minutes, I came across it again. God revealed to me the same Scripture from three different places on the same day. As I was sitting in my dark room, I shed a tear because God was speaking so loud and clear to me. He was telling that I was the salt of the earth, *"but if the salt loses its flavor, how shall it be seasoned? It is then good for nothing but to be thrown out and trampled underfoot by men."* This woke me up and I realized that no matter how hard the hit was from the enemy, I couldn't give up. So, I went back to reading the Bible and praying again.

It took some time before God delivered from those demonic thoughts, but I thank God that he kept me through it all. I had to learn that those thoughts were just lies from the enemy and I didn't have to entertain them anymore. In doing so, I finally overcame the battle of the mind with the power of God fighting for me. As time went on, I had other battles and some shaky moments but through it all, I continued to stand with Jesus. I was not perfect; I didn't cross every "T" or dot every "I" but I loved Jesus and stayed with him.

Now

There will always be more added to my testimony. It grows daily, and I see more of God's goodness each day. I now find myself in a position where the visions and dreams that God has given me are coming to life, and they're closer than ever. I can feel them, I can smell them, and I can see them; they're in reach, and they're manifesting right before my eyes. However, it took much sacrifice and obedience to get here. I had to ignore everyone else's voice to get to God's will for my life. I've learned that you will have to ignore people along the way. People will not always understand what God has called you to do, but you must keep pressing forward because the call is for YOU and not THEM. Don't worry when they tell you that you're too young and that you need to wait; I've literally heard it all over the last 6 years. But it is essential that you know God's voice for yourselves. God speaks to you, people speak to you, and the devil speaks to you. You must know the difference between the three voices. The devil has been trying to knock me off the path that God has set before me. He has spoken to me through people in hopes to deter me from this rail that God has built, but I still stand, and God continues to prevail.

Almost exactly a year ago to the day, God told me to leave my job and go into ministry. Mind you, I had already been serving a lot in ministry for five years, but God was looking for more. God was looking for my sacrifice and my obedience. Despite the difficulties and thoughts of others, I obeyed God. This was the biggest step of faith that I have ever taken in my relationship with God thus far. This last year has not been comfortable, but I know God on a much deeper level since I obeyed his voice. I literally left everything to follow the voice of God. I have sacrificed much, but the Lord has always provided and will continue to provide for my every need. Right now, I stand here excited and ready to win more souls to the Kingdom through the power of God. But I would be nowhere today if I didn't listen to the voice of God when he called me that day, September 25, 2011.

"…Today, if you hear his voice, do not harden your hearts as you did in the rebellion." (Hebrews 3:15 NIV)

CHAPTER 6
THE TEMPTER

Recognizing the Enemy

He is responsible for all the evil that has been seen across the world since the beginning of time. He wages war against believers in the hope that they will stop serving the everlasting God. However, his day of judgment is coming soon, and he will be locked up in the lake of fire for all eternity. Until then, we must learn how to defeat him here on this earth. He goes by the name of Satan. However, the Bible has many names for him such as; "the tempter" (Matthew 4:3), "the devil (Matthew 4:5), "Lucifer" (Isaiah 14:12 NKJV), "The father of lies" (John 8:44), "The great dragon" (Revelation 12:9), "The deceiver of the whole world" (John 8:44), "The god of this age" (2 Corinthians 4:4), "The ancient serpent" (Revelation 20:2) etc. Regardless of the name he goes by, he has one primary goal. That is to separate believers from God. In this chapter, you will learn more about the history of Satan, his goals, his tactics, and how to defeat him.

Who Is He: The History of Satan

Satan first started out in Heaven as one of God's angels. Then one day, pride entered into the heart of Satan, and God kicked him out of Heaven because he said,

"...I will ascend to the heavens; I will raise my throne above the stars of God; I will sit enthroned on the mount of assembly, on the utmost heights of Mount Zaphon. I will ascend above the tops of the clouds; I will make myself like the Most High." (Isaiah 14:13-14 NIV)

Ultimately, Satan, one of God's created angels, wanted to have his own throne and be like God, the Most High God. Satan, being full of himself, thought he could actually overtake God's throne. How crazy is that? He devised what he thought was a master plan to take over, but he fell short, very short. However, being very influential, he was able to convince a third of God's angels to rebel against God. Satan and one-third of the angels were cast out of Heaven. Jesus said, *"...I saw Satan fall like lightning from heaven."* (Luke 10:18 NIV) Satan took a great a fall. As a result of him and the angels' foolish decision, they were given a permanent death sentence that could never be revoked. Even if they wanted to repent, they would never be given a second chance, and they will never escape their final judgment in the lake of fire. All because of one decision to rebel against God. Isn't it crazy how the creation wanted to take over the creator? I can picture Satan and the other angels plotting and planning a way to overthrow God's throne. Satan's pride must've blinded him to the fact that God is all-knowing and all-powerful.

Since Satan will never receive God's redemption, he leads a rebellion against God. He is the leader of darkness, spiritual wickedness, and he has his own demonic Kingdom. Jesus spoke of Satan's kingdom, *"If Satan drives out Satan, he is divided against himself. How then can his kingdom stand?"* (Matthew 12:26 NIV) Jesus lets us know that Satan's kingdom is unified, organized, and an undivided kingdom. But no matter how organized Satan's kingdom is, it will forever lose, and God's kingdom will forever be victorious. But until Satan's great day of judgment, he will keep fighting.

Scriptures on Satan's Judgments

"But you are brought down to the realm of the dead, to the depths of the pit." (Isaiah 14:15 NIV)

"…Depart from me, you who are cursed, into the eternal fire prepared for the devil and his angels." (Matthew 25:41 NIV)

"For if God did not spare angels when they sinned, but sent them to hell, putting them in chains of darkness to be held for judgment." (2 Peter 2:4 NIV)

"And the devil, who deceived them, was thrown into the lake of burning sulfur, where the beast and the false prophet had been thrown. They will be tormented day and night for ever and ever." (Revelation 20:10 NIV)

Satan's Goals and Tactics

Satan's ultimate goal is to pull you away from God and disrupt the call of God on your life. It is important to remain vigilant because he is after you.

"Be alert and of sober mind. Your enemy the devil prowls around like a roaring lion looking for someone to devour." (1 Peter 5:8 NIV)

This Scripture shows us that the devil is literally on the prowl looking for someone to bring back to his kingdom. He doesn't only want you dead, but he wants you to go to hell as well. It's as if his motto is "If I'm going down, so is everyone else." Satan is literally hanging on the edge of a cliff with one hand waiting for his time to come; and while waiting, he will grab anyone he can to take with him. Satan wants you hell-bound, and he will do whatever it takes to get you. I think he may even have a daily quota that his demons must meet. I suggest this because his daily call is to go after you and get you to fall. Satan studies you, plots against you, and pays close attention to the things you like. Each day he's finding new ways to defeat you. He literally has a telescope on you. I picture his demons following you with a pen and studying your every move. Satan and his crew are the demonic paparazzi. They want to find every bit of dirt on you and use it against you. If he catches you always lusting after a particular woman or man, he'll start sending that same type your way, hoping that you bite the bait. It's like fishing; if you want good fish, you must use good bait. Satan will not throw you weak bait or something that you don't like. It wouldn't make sense to send you something that won't get you to bite. You must also learn that the devil will not always use the obvious against you. He is smart enough to realize that he can't just come knocking on your door with a gun in his hand because he knows you are not stupid. Instead of a gun, he will come to you in that size or shape that you like. He will appear to you as an angel of light so that you trust him. When you finally trust him, open your door to him, and turn around, he'll stab you in the back. This is why is he called the deceiver; because he'll trick his way into your home.

Satan Uses Eve Against Adam

One of Satan's most effective weapons is the people that are closest to you. A prime of example of this would be the story of Adam and Eve. When you read the story in Genesis, who was Satan really trying to get to? The answer is Adam because sin could only enter the world through Adam, not Eve. Satan used Eve as a weapon to get to Adam. Satan knew that if he could deceive Eve, Eve could convince Adam to take a bite of the forbidden fruit. And if Adam takes the bite, then sin enters the world and mankind is under a curse. The crazy part is, Adam knew the consequences of eating the forbidden fruit, but his wife was still able to persuade him. Satan wants to blind you from the obvious. He tells you to forget what you know and just take the bite. He'll say things like "you won't really die," "you can just repent," but "just make sure you take this bite." As you know, Adam and Eve both took that bite.

As young believers, it's critical to recognize the tactics of the enemy. The Bible says, *"In order that Satan might not outwit us. For we are not unaware of his schemes."* (2 Corinthians 2:11 NIV) If you are unaware of Satan's schemes, he will outwit you every time. But if you are aware of his plans, he will never outwit you. Just as a football team must study their opponent, so do we have to study our opponent, Satan. When football teams go up against their opponent, they prepare themselves for every possible situation. This includes hours of watching film on their opponent until they know everything about them. Some collegiate football teams spend up 10 hours a week watching film on their opponent. It's time for us, as believers, to start watching film on Satan so that we can defeat him.

How to Defeat the Devil

You must recognize the tactics of the enemy, to learn how to defeat the enemy. First, you must know that you are already victorious and at the end of your story, you will win if you remain in Jesus.

"And the God of peace will crush Satan under your feet shortly." (Romans 16:20 NKJV)

Next, you must know, even as young believers, you have authority over Satan through the spirit of God that resides in you. The Bible says, *"I have given you authority to trample on snakes and scorpions and to overcome all the power of the enemy; nothing will harm you."* (Luke 10:19 NIV) This Scripture is not just for those that have been saved for forty or fifty years; this is for everyone who has

God's spirit in them. The Bible is telling you that you have all power over the devil. That means you must never be afraid of the devil because Jesus is on your side fighting for you. You must also learn to use Scripture against the enemy. Scripture is a great weapon of choice. Jesus fasted in the wilderness forty days and nights, and then Satan appeared to him three times to tempt him. Each time that Jesus was tempted by Satan, He used the Word of God against him and overcame the temptation. The answer to overcoming the enemy is using the Word of God against him.

Lastly, to defeat the enemy and his temptations you must learn to shut the door instead of keeping it open. Don't flirt with the devil because he might get you! When you entertain his offers, he slips through the cracks. When Eve was tempted, she responded with the Word at first, but then she kept the conversation going. When Jesus was tempted, he answered with the Word and then shut the door. Jesus successfully overcame the enemy; Adam and Eve did not. Learn to cut the conversation off with the enemy before it's too late.

I challenge you, as a young believer, to walk in the supernatural power that God has given you over the enemy. If you do that, you will always defeat the devil. Don't worry about Satan attacking you because you must be doing something right! Bishop T.D. Jakes says it best, "When all hell breaks loose in my life, I say I must be doing something right, or the devil wouldn't be fighting me like this." [12]

CHAPTER 7
YOUR PAST

Moving Pass the Past

Your past is the one thing that you cannot take back. It's those decisions that you've made and enjoyed but now regret. If not tamed, your past regrets can weigh you down and make you feel hopeless. Your past is something that you find yourself wrestling with time and time again. Whether you miss it, are still identified by it, or feel guilty about it, there's a constant battle. Ultimately, your past wants you back, but God wants you forward. Which will win, the past or the new you?

Lot's Wife

The Bible is filled with stories about people that could not let go of the past. One of these people will always remain nameless, as the Bible only refers to her as "Lot's wife." (Genesis 19:26) In the book of Genesis, God sends two angels to escort Lot, his wife, and his children out of Sodom because God was going to destroy it. Sodom, along with Gomorrah, were full of wickedness, and God was going to rain down fire and brimstone on the two cities. Just as Lot and his family were safely escorted out of the Sodom, the angel tells them, "...don't look back..." (Genesis 19:17 NIV) Despite the angel's instruction, Lot's wife looked back. When she looked back, she turned into a pillar of salt.

What was it that caused Lots wife to look back? What had such a pull on her, that she couldn't follow a simple instruction? Did she not want to leave her best friends? Was she going to miss the parties? The drugs? The food? What was it? The Bible never tells us exactly what it was, but there was definitely something in Sodom and Gomorrah that caused her to look back.

Sometimes you never make it to the new places that God has intended for you to be because you're too busy looking back. How can God take you somewhere new when you still desire the things of the old? Sodom was a city full of sin and Lot's wife enjoyed it, and that's why she looked back. As believers, we all have our own "Sodoms." Those things that God has freed us from, but deep down inside we still desire them. Has God ever released you from a particular sin? Then once freed, you found yourself wishing you could enjoy that sin just one more time? I wonder if that's how Lot's wife felt. Maybe she just wanted one more taste. What is it in your past that keeps getting you to look back?

The Past is Calling Your Name

Prior to living for Jesus, most people enjoyed their sinful past, which is why it's hard not to look back. When you come to Jesus, it not easy letting go of things that you liked, it's actually very hard. Even after being saved, you still find yourself acting like Lot's wife and looking back.

Some days you even find yourself reminiscing about the sinful things that you used to do. It feels like your sinful past was a part of your glory days. I've had moments since being saved, where I told myself, "If only I wasn't saved, I would..." I said this because at times I missed indulging in the sin that I used to love. It feels like there is a love and hate relationship with our sinful past. At times, you just miss it and want it back because of how much you enjoyed it. And other times you hate it because you know how far away from God it took you.

Knowing our love and hate relationship with sin, the enemy continually tries to draw us back by reminding us of our sinful past. This is why it feels as if your past is always haunting you. Your past seems like this ghost in your ear saying, "come back." This "ghost" usually shows up when you're most vulnerable. As soon as the enemy sees you in a weakened state, he brings up the old you. He does this because he knows the joy you found in sin and he's hoping that you'll latch onto it again. As young believers, we cannot allow our sinful past to become a coping mechanism for hard days. Think about it, when do ex-cigarette smokers usually tend to go back to smoking? Usually after a stressful day. This is the same for believers; we tend to go back to our sinful past ways after stressful days. You do this because you want the sin that you once enjoyed to ease the pressures of life again. So what we tend to do, is go back to the past because it is familiar. It's like someone going back to their ex when they get lonely. They know their ex was not right for them, but they'd rather be with them than be alone. When they're feeling down and need someone to talk to, they call their ex. This is exactly what we do as Christians. When we start feeling down, we call our ex, which is our past.

As believers, we must get through the hard days of life without going back to our former things. One thing that the enemy used to always whisper in my ear was, "Everything was easier before you got saved." I would always hear this after a hard day. However, the enemy never reminded me of God's freedom being better than sin's death grip. You must ignore the voice of the enemy. The devil and your past are just mad because you've moved on from them. They're jealous, and they want you back. You left them behind, and they have become like an obsessive ex that won't stop until they get you. Today we are issuing a restraining order to your past. It no longer has any place in your life, and you will cease to look back because Jesus has made you a new creature.

"Therefore if anyone is in Christ, he is a new creature; the old things passed away; behold, new things have come." (2 Corinthians 5:17 KJV)

People Will Identify You by Your Past

Another unfortunate thing about your past is that people will still identify you by it. When you leave your old lifestyle to live a new one, people will still see the old you. Remember how your friends treated you when you first came to Christ? Remember that awkward moment when you told them, "I don't do that anymore?" Remember that weird look they gave you and how they questioned your seriousness? A lot of times your friends will not believe the converted you because they knew the old you. Your friends are used to the pre-Jesus you, not the saved you.

When I was first saved, I had a lot of friends ask me why I wasn't doing certain things anymore. I explained to them to that I gave my life to Jesus. Some believed it; some didn't. There will always be people that refuse to see the change in you. Some will continue to classify you according to your old nature that wasn't in Christ. Just be sure to tell them that your past doesn't define you, and the old you is dead and gone. Tell them you now have a new resume in Christ that says you are forgiven and changed.

Biblical Example

Some of the first disciples of Jesus Christ had an issue with one of the most influential biblical character's past. The early disciples didn't receive Paul, the Apostle, at first because of his past. Before Paul was an Apostle, his name was Saul, and as you may know, he put to death many of the first Christians. He did this because he was a Pharisee and Pharisees were religious people that believed Jesus was an imposter.

"He made havoc of the church, entering every house, and dragging off men and women, committing them to prison." (Acts 8:3 NKJV)

The pre-Jesus Paul was an evil man who didn't like Christians. However, God still had a plan for Paul despite his past. When Paul was on his way to Damascus to persecute more Christians, God shined a bright light from heaven that blinded him. God told him that a man by the name of Ananias was going to pray for him and his sight would be restored. The Bible tells us what Ananias said to the Lord concerning Paul and his past.

"...I have heard many reports about this man and all the harm he has done to your holy people in Jerusalem. And he has come here with authority from the chief priests to arrest all who call on your name." But the Lord said to Ananias, 'Go! This man is my chosen instrument to proclaim my name to the Gentiles and their kings and to the people of Israel.'" (Acts 9:13-14 NIV)

Ananias was hesitant and fearful about obeying God's instructions because he knew Paul's past. Despite his fear and hesitation, he goes to pray for Paul. Even after Paul gets saved, many of the believers did not accept him because they did not believe he was a changed person. They rejected him and identified him with his past.

"When Saul arrived in Jerusalem, he tried to meet with the believers, but they were all afraid of him. They did not believe he had truly become a believer!" (Acts 9:26 NLT)

"Christians" did not accept Paul because of his past. People inside the church and outside of the church will refuse to accept you because of your past. Don't be discouraged and don't stop; because one of the most well-known biblical characters was rejected for the things he did before coming to Jesus. However, he pressed on and kept doing the work of the Lord. Imagine how many people get saved and then leave the faith each year because no one believes that they are changed. Don't worry if others don't accept you because of the things you've done in the past. God accepts you, despite the things you've done!

Accepting Your Past and Moving On

You may tend to beat yourself up because you regret decisions that you've made. There may be a seemingly never-ending guilt and shame that takes over you. In your mind, you replay your failures, the people you've hurt, and the bad decisions you've made. All the choices you've made that no one knows about, but God. They are your hidden secrets that strip you from peace each and every day. Eventually, these things begin to weigh you down to the point that you give up. At that point, you may start to feel like you cannot move forward anymore because of the guilt that you have. It often surfaces when you're enjoying your day and then randomly you remember the wrongs you've done and the guilt hits you, causing you to lose peace once again. It is hard because you can't even look forward to the future anymore because you keep looking at your past mistakes. I have good news for you! There is hope for you! You don't have to live with the guilt and shame of what you did anymore. From now on do not let your mistakes kill you because Jesus died for every mistake. Every hidden sinful thing, Jesus died for. Jesus has forgiven your sins. Put down the weight of your past and walk in the forgiveness and love of Jesus Christ.

Your Past is Your Testimony

You no longer need to be ashamed of your past. The Apostle Paul spoke of the terrible things he did before he knew Jesus. He opened his life up and showed us that he wasn't always an Apostle, but that he once was a terrible person. It's okay that you have a past. EVERYONE has a past. Embrace the goodness of God and how he delivered you from your past. Every time you give the testimony of your past, you're giving the glory back to God. Too many young believers hide how good God has been to them. When I got saved at the age of 18, I had a lot of confessing to do to my parents because I had a testimony that the world needed to hear.

I'll never forget the night I went into my parent's room and told them of the wrongs that I had done. I revealed things that I had hid from them for several years. I didn't want to tell them, but I did so because I knew my testimony was for the world. I knew that God would use my shortcomings to help someone else. Your testimonies are weapons that deliver people. Don't be afraid or embarrassed by your testimony! People love you when you are transparent about your past because it shows them that you are human too. Be open with people, so you can win them to Christ. How can you be used by God to "snatch your friends out of the fire" when you're too afraid to tell them how you got out of the fire? Your past shortcomings are going to save someone's soul.

New Creature

Remember, in Christ, you are a new creature, and your past does not define you! You are not who you used to be! Your slate has been wiped clean because Jesus makes all things new! Your sins are no longer scarlet, but they are white as snow. The past will no longer hold you back!

CHAPTER 8
MASK ON, MASK OFF

Who Are You Really?

Mask on, mask off, what's with all of these masks? And why are so many people hiding behind them? Well, the purpose of a mask is to conceal someone's identity. When a mask is on, you can hide the real you and be someone you're not.

Think about it, burglars and robbers wear masks to hide their identity so that they can live a life without repercussions. A mask allows you to live a double life. Sometimes, as believers, we put on masks so that we can be someone different; constantly flip-flopping between different masks for different crowds. Who do I want to be today? We tend to treat our Christianity like a masquerade ball. Be whoever you want to be because your face is covered.

False Identity

A mask can also be seen as a false identity. Why? Because we're putting up a front and putting on a fake persona. Every Christian has been guilty of disguising themselves at one time or another because we didn't want to be classified as a Christian. However, when we do this, we act just like society and not as followers of Christ.

Currently, in society, a lot of people are struggling with false identities. Instead of keeping it real, they'd rather pretend to be someone they're not. The reality-based documentary television series, "Catfish," is a good example of this. In the show, people pretend to be someone they're not in hopes of finding true love over the internet. It is crazy that someone would create a name, steal someone's picture, and pretend to live a life that they really don't, all for love! Unfortunately, a lot of things in our culture are just not real. People alter pictures of themselves, inject themselves, and even have surgeries because they're not content with their identity. Sadly, the Christian world has gotten caught up in this system of false identities.

If you were to scroll down your Facebook page right now, someone has probably posted this today, "People just need to be 100 (Insert Emoji)!" I don't blame them though, because who wants to be around someone that doesn't keep it real? It's hard to respect someone who pretends to be someone else. False identities are everywhere, and we must make sure that we are not a part of that system. I know society doesn't like you because you're different but don't hide who you are. If you're a Christian, be a Christian. We should no longer be ashamed of the Gospel that saves!

"For I am not ashamed of the gospel, for it is the power of God for salvation to everyone who believes..." (Romans 1:16 NKJV)

Unashamed Christians Don't Wear Masks.

As followers of Jesus, we must not be a mask switcher. Just because we're around nonbelievers doesn't mean that we can put on our less of a Jesus mask either. You know that mask! It's the mask where we refrain from praying over our food or where we engage in certain conversations because non-believers are surrounding us. I'm guilty of this. A couple years ago I went out to eat with my co-workers, and once I received my food, I did a two-second prayer over my food so that no one saw me praying. I did this because I didn't feel like hearing someone say, "You pray over your food?" "Are you a Christian?" It is sad to admit, but sometimes as believers, we become ashamed.

I do wonder if it breaks God's heart when he sees us acting like we don't know him. Think about it for a second. How would you feel if your significant other acted like they didn't know you? What if behind your back they didn't claim you as theirs because they were ashamed of you? Your feelings would probably be hurt and your heart would be broken. I know this because we live in a society where your boyfriend or girlfriend will get upset with you if you don't update your relationship status fast enough on Facebook. There's a complete double standard here. We expect our significant other to never be ashamed of us but at times we're ashamed of God.

It's crazy that we expect God to accept us when we're ashamed of Him. It blows my mind that God still loves us when we profess Jesus in our closet but in public, we are ashamed. In our prayer room, it's "Jesus, I love you," but outside it's "Jesus, I don't know you!"

Us Christians can be the greatest actors. We play roles so good that we deserve an Oscar. We get so caught up in playing church that we forget to actually be the church. Living for Jesus can't be practiced only when it's convenient. It must be done 24/7 – 365 days a year. Let's not become believers who talk the talk and don't walk the walk. We often think that we're okay with God because of how well we talk and how well we church. However, you can go to church all day and still be far from God. Let's lose the masks.

"These people...honor me with their lips, but their hearts are far from me." (Matthew 15:8 NKJV)

Be Comfortable in Your Christian Skin

Ultimately, we must get to the heart of the mask issue. Many people are just not comfortable in their Christian skin. Sadly, when you're uncomfortable and insecure, a mask comes in handy. It's just like makeup. Makeup can be used to blanket insecurities, and a mask is worn to blanket an insecure Christian. I once saw a picture buzzing through social media. It was a two-sided picture with the same lady on both sides. On one side, it was her face without makeup, and you could see all of her acne scars, which covered 95% of her face. On the other side, her face was completely covered with makeup, and she looked like a different person. You literally couldn't tell that they were the same person. That's how we become with our Christian skin. We cover up with makeup, masks, and personalities to the point that people can't even see that we are a Christian. God is telling us to get rid of it all and to be comfortable in our Christian skin.

How can God use us for His glory when we're insecure in our Christian skin? I remember being ashamed of my Christian skin. When I finally became comfortable and embraced who I was, I began to see God speak through me a lot more. At work, I was always extra cautious about Jesus talk because I didn't want to offend people. When I finally started to speak up, I learned that some people were actually very curious about Jesus. Some conversations I had with co-workers became moments of healing and understanding as to who Jesus is. Some people have never been invited to church or had someone pray for them. When you are comfortable in your Christian skin, there's no telling of all the marvelous things God can do in the lives of your peers. God wants to save your co-workers and your classmates. Don't put your Jesus identity on the shelf at work or school.

Consistency Is a Major Key

We live in a society where people are looking for consistency, especially from the church. Could it be that the lack of consistency is the reason why our unsaved co-workers, friends, and family aren't taking us seriously? We can no longer be one person on Facebook and another person face to face. We have unsaved friends who see our Jesus posts and have a preconceived notion as to who they believe we are as a Christian. They expect us to act like a Christian and they hold us to a higher standard. What they don't expect, is for us to act as they do. If we act the same way that they do, they will conclude that there is no difference between us, the Christian and themselves, the Non-Christians. That's why it's critical that our Facebook posts match up with our lifestyle. We can't just be a Facebook Christian.

There's no reason why people shouldn't know that we're believers. This is not something that should be discovered through a third party or when they befriend us on social media. The Jesus in us should have already been recognized by them. They should have already seen the light in us. The problem is that many people do not wear Jesus on their sleeve. You can never win the lost acting like the lost. It's time for us, as young believers, to come back to consistency with God and people. Our lives inside and outside of the church should be parallel. We do not need any more imposters. We need to be real and stand up.

Do a quick self-analysis and ask yourself these questions.

1   Who do the church people say you are?

2   Who do your friends say you are?

3   Who are you behind closed doors?

4   Who does Jesus say you are?

The answer to all four of these questions should be the same. When you identify with Jesus, there should be Jesus characteristics visible throughout your life. It would be a shame if someone close you didn't know that you were saved. Strive for consistency.

I will always remember a very inconsistent moment of mine. A couple months after I was saved, I ran into a friend while riding the bus. As we were talking, he asked me a question about something I did in my past. Instead of telling him that I'm saved, and that I don't do that anymore, I gave in and answered the question about my past. I remember feeling uncomfortable about answering the question, but I also remember being too afraid to stand for Jesus. In this Christian life, you will be in some of the most awkward situations. You will feel enormous pressure, but never forget who you are. One thing that people will always remember and respect about you is your consistency for Jesus.

Never be afraid to be a public Christian. Your Christian hood should be on display for the whole world to see. In the book of Daniel, there was a decree set that no one could pray to a god or any human being for 30 days expect King Darius, Daniel's response was clear.

"Now when Daniel learned that the decree had been published, he went home to his upstairs room where the windows opened toward Jerusalem. Three times a day he got down on his knees and prayed, giving thanks to his God, just as he had done before." (Daniel 6:10 NIV)

Daniel displayed true consistency and faithfulness to God, no matter the price. Being a public Christian comes with much persecution, but it also comes with much joy. This is a joy that no one can take away from you, not even death. I challenge you to be like Daniel. Do not give in to the pressures of being someone that you're not. Be true to yourself and love God in public and in private. You don't need to wear a mask, just be faithful to God. It gets challenging, especially at work, school, and in other settings but it is worth it. You will find joy in standing for Jesus. Will the real SAINTS please stand up? #NoMoreMasks

CHAPTER 9
DON'T FALL

It's Not Worth It

It seems as if each month there's a new Christian leader experiencing a major fall. Scandal after scandal is all you seem to see in the Christian news media. When you go to some Christian websites the very first thing that you see is, **"The pastor of ___, was just caught having an affair with his secretary. It is believed that the affair has been going on for several years now. We tried to get hold of the church, but they refused to comment."**

I know that I'm not the only one who gets tired of seeing these articles. Every time a Christian leader falls, the whole world looks at us and calls us all hypocrites. Just the other day on Facebook, I saw that an extended family member of mine, (very extended) posted that all Christians are hypocrites. I really wanted to respond to her Facebook post, but I didn't want to stir up anything. But it made me wonder, what can we do to stop this deadly epidemic of Christian leaders falling? We must discover a way to prevent these catastrophic falls from happening. I understand that not one person on this earth is perfect, *"...all have sinned and fall short of the glory of God."* (Romans 3:23 NIV) However, I do believe that God did not intend for us take significant falls and have scandals. In this life, we will always have shortcomings, but we don't need to take a major fall. We must learn how not to fall because we are the generation that everyone is looking at. So, we must start setting an example for the generations to come, and it starts with our conduct as a Christian.

Bible Characters That Fell

The Bible doesn't hesitate to point out believers that took major falls. I used to wonder why God would reveal all of their business and bad conduct to us. I mean, it has to be embarrassing for everyone to know everything that you did. If you fall today, most people may forget it about it in 5-10 years. But for those whose fell in the Bible, their stories stay alive forever. The Bible characters have generations of people seeing all of the dirt that they did. However, I do believe that God reveals their downfalls to us, so that we don't fall to the same things.

Some Biblical Characters That Fell

- Adam and Eve: Forbidden fruit in the Garden of Eden.
- Noah: Got so drunk that his children saw him naked.
- Lot: Got so drunk that he slept with his own daughters.
- King David: Adultery, murder, and deception.
- King Solomon: Women and idols.
- Samson: Delilah and disobedience.

Funny thing is that we look up to most of these biblical characters on this list and we honored them for the great things that they did. Nevertheless, a lot of them did some messy things that we don't have to follow. Sometimes we think that falls aren't that serious because someone may have a great story of redemption. I want to let you know that not every fall ends with a prodigal-son-returns-story. There are a lot of people who never recover from great falls.

Consequences of A Great Fall (Like Father, Like Son)

One Bible character that fell very hard was King Solomon, who was the son of King David. Solomon was a great man of God. He was so close to God that God gave him divine wisdom and knowledge. Solomon's wisdom gave him all the answers to life. He was literally the talk of the world because of his great wisdom. He was rich in wisdom and in money with a net worth in the billions. But one day, he found himself in a situation that was very displeasing to God. King Solomon began doing things that took him outside of the will of God. He was no longer the Godly man that he used to be; he actually became the opposite. Solomon made a 180-degree flip and went from building holy altars for God to building altars for false gods. Solomon, who once worshipped the one and true living God, was now worshiping false gods because his "foreign" wives led him astray.

When you look at the context of Solomon's story, you learn that he was instructed to not marry certain foreign women from particular nations, but Solomon did it anyways. God had forewarned him that these foreign women would turn his heart to their gods. However, Solomon ignored the warnings and followed after his own heart's desire. Solomon willingly disobeyed God, which is the ultimate recipe for a great fall.

Solomon's Warning

"...You must not intermarry with them, because they will surely turn your hearts after their gods." Nevertheless, Solomon held fast to them in love." He had seven hundred wives of royal birth and three hundred concubines, and his wives led him astray. As Solomon grew old, his wives

turned his heart after other gods, and his heart was not fully devoted to the Lord his God..." (1 Kings 11:2-4 NIV)

As a result of Solomon's disobedience, he had great consequences. The story shows us how God tears away the majority of the Israelite's kingdom from Solomon's kingship and gives it to one of his subordinates. But since God loved King David (Solomon's Father), God waited until Solomon's son's reign to execute the judgment. In other words, God was firing Solomon as Israel's King; he just didn't have to experience it, his son had to. This is an excellent example of how sin can affect you, your children and those around you. I know I would feel awful if my sin affected my seed.

Ultimately, the main consequence that Solomon had was separation from God's presence at that time. There's nothing worse than being out of God's will and knowing that you're doing wrong. It's believed that at some point, King Solomon may have repented because of his closing statements in the book of Ecclesiastes. Whether he fully repented or not; it is still essential that you get back up when you fall. In this life, you may fall tremendously, and the whole world may know the wrong that you did, but that shame is not comparable to eternal separation from God. Could you imagine being eternally separated from God? Could you imagine wanting God, but not being able to have him no matter how much you cried out? That's why it's important that we get right with God while still have time. Never let the thoughts others keep you from crawling back to God. Repent while you still can. A great example of a man of God who fell but repented was King Solomon's Father, King David.

King David (Solomon's Father)

At one point, God called King David, *"...a man after his own heart..."* (1 Samuel 13:14 NIV) It is hard to imagine that someone after "God's own heart" could take a significant fall. King David loved God tremendously, but he did do a few unthinkable things that angered God. It all started one day when King David should've been at war with his army, but instead, he chose to stay home. While at home in his palace, King David got out of bed and walked to the roof.

"...From the roof he saw a woman bathing. The woman was very beautiful, and David sent someone to find out about her. The man said, 'She is Bathsheba, the daughter of Eliamand the wife of Uriah the Hittite.' Then David sent messengers to get her. She came to him, and he slept with her." (2 Samuel 11:2-4 NIV)

This was an incredible dilemma. King David, a man after God's own heart, just did the unthinkable and had sex with another man's wife. As the story continues, you find out that David knocked-up Bathsheba and she was now set to have his baby in nine months. Upon learning of her pregnancy, David makes a couple desperate attempts to cover-up his sin instead of just coming clean. When you try to cover your sin, your hands will just get dirtier. Unfortunately, David had to learn this lesson.

The first thing that David does to conceal his sin was to call Bathsheba's husband, Uriah, home from war. David does this hoping that Uriah would go home and sleep with his wife Bathsheba so that it would look like Uriah impregnated her. However, this plan fails because Uriah doesn't feel right going home to his wife, while everyone else is at war away from their wives. So, the following day, David gets Uriah drunk, in hopes that he would now go home and sleep with his wife, Bathsheba. But this plan fails too because Uriah still won't go home. Both plans failed, so finally the next day, David writes a letter for Uriah to deliver to the armies' commander, Joab.

"...Put Uriah out in front where the fighting is fiercest. Then withdraw from him so he will be struck down and die." (2 Samuel 11:15 NIV)

The crazy part about this story is that David had Uriah carry that very letter to his commander. Uriah literally carried the letter that contained his death sentence. Uriah was so loyal to David that he could be trusted not to open the sealed letter. If Uriah had opened it, he would've read David's plot to kill him, but Uriah didn't open it, and as a result, he and many others in the army were killed. David was now responsible for several deaths, including Uriah, because of his one decision.

Once news hit home about Uriah's death, Bathsheba mourned for her husband, Uriah, that was just murdered by the man who impregnated her. Yet, Bathsheba isn't a widow for long because King David calls for her and marries her. David is probably on cloud-nine because he just had a baby with a beautiful woman, murdered his new wife's husband, and got away with it.

However, just when David thought he was in the clear, God revealed it through the prophet Nathan. The prophet Nathan went to David and gave him a riddle about a man who took something that wasn't his. Interestingly, David didn't realize that the riddle was about him, and instead, he became angered and said, "...As surely as the Lord lives, the man who did this must die!" (2 Samuel 12:5 NIV)

The Prophet Nathan proceeds to tell him, "...You are the man!" (2 Samuel 12:7 NIV) God then speaks a word of judgment on David and his household because of the evil that he did to Uriah. Upon hearing the judgment, David confesses his sin and God decides not to kill him, but he instead strikes dead David and Bathsheba's new baby boy. One bad decision to sleep with Bathsheba and kill Uriah, impacted his household tremendously in the days to come, just like God said it would.

We can learn a lot from David's story. Before a great fall. you always have two choices, choose right or choose wrong. When David saw Bathsheba bathing in the moonlight, he should've turned his head and gone back to bed. As believers, we must think before we make a decision that can impact the rest of our life. Someone reading this right now, may have been tempted and is close to making a decision that would result in a great fall. I want to encourage you today to not do it because it's just not worth it. Don't make the same mistakes that these biblical characters made. Before making a horrible decision, think about all that God has planned for you. If you are contemplating on making a terrible decision, the following Scripture is for you.

"What no eye has seen, what no ear has heard, and what no human mind has conceived¾the things God has prepared for those who love him." (1 Corinthians 2:9 NIV)

God has a great plan for your future, and it would be a shame if you mess it up with one dumb decision. And if you have already fallen, there is still hope for you! You just have to repent and get up again. A good example of repentance is found in Psalm 51 when David repents for his actions with Bathsheba and Uriah. Never forget that God can restore you, just like he did David. Don't be like Judas, when he fell, just repent, don't kill yourself. Trust me; God will forgive you!

Encouragement and Prayer for the Fallen

If you're reading this right now and you have fallen, it's important to get back up. No matter what you did wrong, God can cleanse you. God can turn your story around. When the prodigal son left the father's house and did evil, God not only received him back home, but He ran to him. God is running to you right now, and He's ready to hold you in His arms. God still has a plan for you! His love for you never changed! In Jesus' name, I pray that God would restore you, heal you and make you whole right now.

Four Tools to Prevent a Fall

1. Examine yourself

It is essential that you know your own flaws and weaknesses. Give yourself an honest evaluation about your struggles. When you identify your weaknesses, you learn the situations that aren't good for you and what your potential falling points are. For example, if you struggle with getting drunk, a bar isn't the place for you to be.

2. Don't ignore God's warning signs

Whenever you're tempted to make a big mistake, God always provides a way out. "...*God is faithful; he will not let you be tempted beyond what you can bear. But when you are tempted, he will also provide a way out so that you can endure it.*" (1 Corinthians 10:13 NIV) Think of a time when you were close to doing something that you had no business doing. Did someone close to you text or call you randomly just before you did it? If so, that was God giving you a minute to think twice about your next decision. I can think of several times when I was getting ready to do something wrong, and then randomly I received a call or text from my mom. There have even been times that people had dreams of me doing ungodly things, that I was actually doing. These were all warning signs from God. Isn't the love of Jesus such a great thing? When you're about to get yourself in trouble, he provides a door of escape for you!

3. Be on guard

Remember growing up as kid and being told to look both ways when you cross the street? We must do the same thing in our spiritual walk. If the streets aren't clear, don't cross. When you're cautious, look both ways and use your mind, you'll avoid getting hit. Don't jaywalk in the spirit. It's always best to err on the side of caution, especially when it comes to sin. If it doesn't look right or feel right, it's probably not right. It's important to analyze all situations. You don't need to be awkward and put up a million walls around you, but simply be on guard.

4. Remember your destiny

Lastly, it's important to remember who you are and what God has called you to do. Ask yourself if those five minutes of pleasure are worth a great fall. There's nothing here on earth that is worth risking your destiny. We need a generation to be scandal free. We need to make the media for a great revival, not for another scandal. May the power of God keep you from falling young soldier!

"Now unto him that is able to keep you from falling, and to present you faultless before the presence of his glory with exceeding joy" (Jude 1:24 KJV)

CHAPTER 10
SEND ME

I'm Ready

We are now on the final chapter of Young and Saved entitled, "Send Me." Do you remember when you told the Lord, "Send me, I'm ready to do your will?" It was probably an exciting moment for you. I can imagine you with a nice big smile saying, "Lord, I'm ready to take on the world, I'll do anything that you want me to do." However, you probably learned that the "Send Me" process was much harder than what you expected. It's a very rigorous, tiring, and faith-walking process. Nevertheless, it's a beautiful one. I remember being a new convert and wanting to do anything and everything for the Lord. Then suddenly I was put into this process called "Send Me." I soon learned that we all must go through this process and that it comes with joy, sorrow, disappointment, impatience, hardships, but most importantly, God's continued faithfulness. You learn who God is in the "Send Me" process. In this chapter you will learn about the six-step process that takes place in your life when you tell the Lord, "Send Me, I'm Ready."

Surrender

When you say to the Lord, "Send Me," you must be willing to surrender your entire life. This can be challenging because surrendering your life requires you to actually give up your life. True surrender gives Jesus the full authority to be Lord. When Jesus is your Lord, He is your master, captain, and chief. You're literally giving Jesus the keys to your life. Before God sends you anywhere, He will first look for your keys. God cannot send an un-surrendered person to do His work. You cannot hold onto to your life and follow Jesus at the same time. It's either all of you or none of you.

Sacrifice

The next step in the process is sacrifice. The call of God on your life will require you to leave things that you love, behind. The things that are so dear to your heart may have to go. Sacrifice is a hard pill to swallow because sometimes the dreams that you've had since your childhood must go. That lifelong goal that you felt was your purpose on this earth may not be a part of God's will for your life. Every goal, dream, and vision that is out of God's will, will have to go. At times, this will be very difficult, but it gets easier when you understand that God has something greater in store for you. I remember seeing an image on the internet once with a little girl holding tight onto a small teddy bear, and standing in front of the little girl was Jesus with one hand out asking for her teddy bear. However, behind Jesus' back he had a huge teddy bear. The little girl had to sacrifice her little teddy bear for something bigger and better. Sometimes you hold onto things so tightly when God is telling you to let it go because he has something better for you!

In the Bible, a perfect example of sacrifice is found in the life of John the Baptist. This man was the forerunner who prepared the way for Jesus Christ. John the Baptist had no career or wife. Instead, he sacrificed his entire life to preach the gospel of repentance. He was a man that lived in the wilderness surviving on wild locusts and honey. He didn't have gold garments. Instead, he had camel's hair as his wardrobe. Why did John the Baptist live a life like that? Because he knew the call of God on his life was much more important than any dream, vision, or goal of his own. He gave up everything just to satisfy the Lord. If God called you to live a life like John the Baptist or Jesus' first disciples, would you say yes?

"And Jesus, walking by the Sea of Galilee, saw two brothers, Simon called Peter, and Andrew his brother, casting a net into the sea; for they were fishermen. Then He said to them, 'Follow Me, and I will make you fishers of men.' They immediately left their nets and followed Him." (Matthew 4:18-20 NKJV)

What I love about that Scripture is that the first disciples didn't ask Jesus any questions; they just immediately left their nets (careers) to follow Jesus. They didn't say, "Lord, we want to keep being fishermen," they just dropped their nets and followed the Lord. God is calling you to drop your nets and follow him. God's will is stronger than any earthly value stored in your nets. I am not saying you should quit your job and preach the gospel tomorrow. But, I am saying that if God does call you to leave your job, certain friends, or whatever it may be, do it right away. Peter and Andrew sacrificed everything before they knew anything. Jesus never gave them a 5-step plan on how everything was going to play out. He just said, "Follow me," and they dropped their nets and followed him.

*"Then another disciple said to Him, '**Lord, first let me go and bury my father**.' But Jesus told him, 'Follow me, and let the dead bury their own dead.'"* (Matthew 8:21-22 NKJV)

It may seem harsh for Jesus to say, "Let the dead bury their own dead," but Jesus could see that the man was not ready to follow him. Had he been ready to follow Jesus, he would've dropped

YOUNG AND SAVED: LIVING IN A WORLD THAT'S NOT LIKE YOU

everything like Peter and Andrew. There was also a rich young ruler who Jesus told, *"...sell your possessions and give to the poor, and you will have treasure in heaven. Then come, follow me."* (Matthew 19:21 NIV) Unfortunately, the man decided not to follow Jesus because he had many riches. Your walk with Jesus requires a great sacrifice, but in that sacrifice, there's an even greater reward and joy that no one can steal from you. People around you will call you crazy for giving up everything to follow Jesus. It's a good thing that we don't follow people; we follow Jesus. Not everyone will understand what God has called you to do.

If Abraham lived today, imagine how people would feel about him going to the mountain to sacrifice his son Isaac because God told him to do it. If that happened in the 21st century, Christians would call Abraham crazy, and he would be put in jail. Regardless of how anyone felt in Abraham's day though, he obeyed the voice of God and went to sacrifice his son. He was willing to sacrifice the very same thing that God had promised him. Then, just as Abraham was getting ready to sacrifice his son Isaac with a knife, God provided a ram in the bush as the sacrifice instead. Since Abraham was obedient and willing to sacrifice the very thing he loved, God rewarded him greatly. I want to encourage you to be obedient to God and surrender all because Jesus is your all. There's a guaranteed return for your sacrifice. Sacrifice is an essential part of God's pruning process for your life. Before God sends you, He requires a sacrifice.

Preparation

When being sent anywhere, you must first be prepared. How can one be sent to do the work of the Lord without first being prepped? That's why, before God sends you; he prepares you. Think about it, before you take an SAT, you prepare yourself for the test. If you don't prepare yourself, you will fail. I can't even count how many times in my life I didn't prepare for a test, and I flunked it. I'm sure many of you have that same story. The times when you had all year to prepare yourself for one test, but instead of preparing yourself, you messed around. And when that exam score came back, you weren't happy. God deals with you in a similar fashion. If you refuse to get prepared and study for the next level, you will get held back and redo the same year over again. That's currently happening in the body of Christ a lot. God has placed some of us on a redo-cycle because we are not getting ready for the next grade. Don't be lazy, be a good student in your season of preparation because God will not send you to a place that you're not prepared for.

An example of someone in the Bible who was properly prepared was King David. God started David's training while he was a little shepherd boy tending to the needs of the smelly sheep. While tending to the sheep, David would sharpen his slingshot skills by killing off a bear and a lion. Little did David know, but that same slingshot was going to be used one day to kill Goliath, one of Israel's biggest threats. David prepared alone, with no one watching and David defeated Goliath with everyone watching. What David learned in secret became known to the public. Don't dismiss your training ground because no one is watching. Preparation is not always public, but instead, it's private and lonely.

It's also good to know that the preparation process may take a while, so you must be patient. David was anointed and selected in his youth to become the King of Israel. But David was not actually put into position as King until almost 20 years after being anointed. That's a huge gap. Those 20 years were needed so that David could get prepared and succeed at being the King, unlike Saul. It's not easy to wait, especially when you know that your destiny is great, but you still must get prepared!

There's such a great a calling on your life, and that's why your season of preparation is hard. A great task ahead comes with great training behind. It's important that you get ready for what's ahead of you. The season of preparation can get incredibly frustrating, and it's easy to become impatient because we tend to want everything right away. But be patient, and don't neglect your season of preparation. God will not send you until you're ready. David had a choice while tending to the smelly sheep, be lazy or get prepared. He chose to prepare. Therefore he succeeded at being King.

Purging

When God is prepping you, he also purging you. How can you go somewhere new with old dirty ways? It's not possible; God must purge you from anything that can ruin you in your next season of life. What good is it to have all the credentials, licenses, degrees and look nice on the outside but be filthy on the inside? There are many Christians who seem like they have it all together but inside there are some deeply rooted issues, that need to be cleaned out. God wants you to look good on the inside and the outside. So to be clean inside, God must purge you. He purges you because some things in you can't go to where you're called to be.

For example, if God called you to be an accountant, but you have a problem stealing money, would it make sense for God to put you in that position right away? Absolutely not, because why would God put you around money knowing that you have a problem stealing it? God would first purge you of your desires to steal money so that you can be the best accountant. Everything that is not good in you must go. Getting purged will not feel good because you're fighting against deep desires that have been rooted in you since childhood. But you can't move forward in the "Send Me" process without being purged first!

Think about it, when you catch a fish, do you throw it on the grill and eat right away? No, because it is unclean and full of filth. When you catch a fish, you gut it and clean it, so that you can eat it. Just like a fish needs to be cleaned before being served, we need to be cleaned as well. Before the fish was in your hands, it was filled with disgusting things that you don't want in your system. Before we came to Jesus, we had a lot of disgusting things in our system that were not suitable for Kingdom work. Many of us came with years of sin built up within us, for that purpose we can never neglect the purging process. Ask the Lord to clean you and make you ready for what's next in your life.

"Purge me with hyssop, and I shall be clean: wash me, and I shall be whiter than snow." (Psalm 51:7 NKJV)

Desire

You have surrendered, sacrificed, prepared, been purged; now desires must change! Without desire, it's hard to be effective in the Kingdom. Through this whole process, you should have a desire to do the things of God. Your desire is one of the first things that God changes within you. There is a tradeoff that takes place; God gives you new desires, and you give him your old ones. You ever notice how once you got saved, some of your ambitions changed? It seemed like a switch flipped in your mind, and you started to desire Godly things. That's because during this process, God is literally transforming your mind and changing your desires! And when you desire to do God's work, you'll work even harder for the Kingdom.

Have you ever had a job at a company that you didn't enjoy? Remember how you didn't care about going further in the company because you hated the job? And since you had no desire for the job, you probably didn't clock in on time because you didn't want to be there. Simply, you just weren't as effective as you could've been because you didn't care for the job. Now think about the time you had a job that you actually enjoyed. I'm sure going to work was no longer a problem for you, you showed up on time and worked hard because your desire was to be there. See the difference? Less desire equals less work done. More desire equals more work done.

God can get a lot more out of you when there is a desire in you. Desire is also good for you because it will carry you through the hard times. The "Send Me" process is hard, but your desire will help you get through. As a believer, you will have many troubles, but your fire and passion becomes your driving force. It is like someone wanting to lose weight. The working out, eating healthy, and eating less will not "always" be fun; and some days you will want to give up. But your desire for a dream body is what keeps you going. And the moment that you get on the scale and realize that you lost 10 pounds, you become filled with joy. Guess what it was it that carried you through those dreadful workouts and healthy eating habits? YOUR DESIRE.

Growing up I loved playing football, but I hated summer practices. Summer practice was awful because we didn't play any games we just worked-out incredibly hard. And on the scorching 100 plus degree-days, we would run steep dirt hills. Dirt would literally fill our lungs as we were running. Sweat would drip from our bodies, and everyone around is coughing, choking and puking. It's really an awful sight to see.

However, football was my desire, and that's what got me through those dreadful summer workouts. Desire pushed me to wake up at 5am for practice and then come back again at noon for another two and half hour practice. And when I was running those dirt hills in a 100 plus degree weather, I knew that it would be worth it in the end because my desire for the game was great. I had a coach once who gave us this team motto, "Desire, Confidence, Love of the game." This has always stuck with me because you're nothing without desire. Your walk comes with pain, but your desire will push you through to the very end. One day you will lay down every weight and see Jesus face to face.

GO

Finally, I want to encourage you to GO! You've read about surrender, sacrifice, preparation, purging, and desire but now it's time to GO. Nothing happens until you take those first steps and go. Your GO will not be easy, but it will be worth it. There will be roadblocks and things that come up against you. At times you will feel overlooked and underappreciated, and you will ask yourself if this is really worth it? You will even start to wonder if you're anointed enough for the task that God has placed before you. Thoughts will begin to penetrate your mind telling you just to leave it all and give up. Your friends, church family, and family will not always see what God has placed in you, but never lose your go. And those days when you just get tired and feel ready to throw in the towel, just keep going and don't stop. Fight this fight until the very end! Never stop going.

Throughout this process, God will always have your back, and you will never be alone. I can honestly say, that through the "Send Me" process God never left me nor forsook me, he was by my side the entire time. If He was by my side, I know he'll be by your side as well. All God wants is our yes and our go! If I had not given God my yes and my go, I wouldn't be writing this book right now. I shared in the "My Testimony" chapter that God told me to GO and leave my job and do more in ministry. Mind you, I had just graduated from college, was recently married and my wife and I were living with my parents while trying to save money. When God said, "Go," it didn't make sense in the natural because I had nothing lined up. Matter fact, I needed more money and God was telling me to leave the money that I was making. For a short time, I felt stuck because I didn't know what I was going to do. But I did know God's voice. So, despite not knowing the steps, I went, and I gave God my go, and I'm so glad that I did.

The "Send Me" process has taught me a lot. I would do all over again because now I know God on a much more deeper level than

I ever imagined. It wasn't easy surrendering my whole life. It was even harder to sacrifice the things that I loved. My season of preparation felt like forever.

And being purged, really hurt because I had lifelong tendencies that had to go. Changing my desire was challenging too because I wanted to stick to my own ways. Going was even harder because at times I felt lost, but God was actually guiding my steps. It is so much better to be in God's will than your own. It's so much better to please God instead of man.

Give God your yes and your whole heart. He will equip you for every single task. Make sure that you "Go" even when it doesn't make sense. Keep going when the world rises up against you and hates you. It is not easy being young and saved; it's a real dogfight. But Jesus gives you the power to overcome and win. Remember, you've already won the battle in Christ, and you will not be defeated as long you as you keep going. Don't let the world change you, change it. God has called you to do great things for him, so do it, be young and saved.

"...In the world you shall have tribulation: but be of good cheer; I have overcome the world." (John 16:33 NKJV)

Thank you for taking this journey with me.

#YoungAndSaved

ENDNOTES

1   James C. McPartland and Ami Klin, "Asperger's syndrome," *Adolescent Medicine Clinics*, PMID 17030291 (2006)

2   Roemer, L., & Nagashima, K. (Directors), Muller, R. (Writer), & Rankin Jr, A., & Bass, J. (Producers). (1964). *Rudolph the Red-Nosed Reindeer*[Motion picture]. United States: Rankin Bass Productions.

3   "I gave up everything for my boyfriend and now that he's left, I'm desolate," *The Stanton Peele Addiction Website*, Accessed August 25, 2017, http://www.peele.net/faq/desolate.html

4   Vera Papisova, "Find Out When Most Teens Are Losing Their Virginity," *Teen Vogue*, September 30, 2015, http://www.teenvogue.com/story/teens-losing-virginity-age

5   Michael F. Haverluck, "Survey: Alarming rate of Christian men look at porn, commit adultery," *One News Now Website*, October 9, 2014, https://www.onenewsnow.com/culture/2014/10/09/survey-alarming-rate-of-christian-men-look-at-porn-commit-adultery

6   Joseph Henry Thayer, A Greek–English Lexicon of the New Testament (New York: Harper & Brothers, 1889), pp. 79-80

7   "Inappropriate Dancing," *Speaking Sound Doctrine Website*, Accessed August 25, 2017, http://www.speakingsounddoctrine.com/Dancing.htm

8   Ibid.

9   "Fact About Weed Addiction – Decide For Yourself If Marijuana Is Addictive," *Addict Help Website*, Accessed August 25, 2017, https://www.addict-help.com/cannabis/can-you-get-addicted-to-weed

10   Ibid.

11   "What does the Bible say about sorcery?," *Got Question Ministries Website,* May 5, 2013,
https://www.gotquestions.org/Bible-sorcery.html

12   Bishop T.D. Jakes, "Know Your Enemy," *YouTube Video,*
Accessed August 25, 2017,
https://www.youtube.com/watch?v=mxEBMVRcLrI

BIBLIOGRAPHY

Addict Help Website. "Fact About Weed Addiction – Decide For Yourself If Marijuana Is Addictive." Accessed August 25, 2017. https://www.addict-help.com/cannabis/can-you-get-addicted-to-weed.

Got Question Ministries Website. "What does the Bible say about sorcery?" May 5, 2013. https://www.gotquestions.org/Bible-sorcery.html.

Haverluck, Michael F. "Survey: Alarming rate of Christian men look at porn, commit adultery." *One News Now Website.* October 9, 2014. https://www.onenewsnow.com/culture/2014/10/09/survey-alarming-rate-of-christian-men-look-at-porn-commit-adultery.

Jakes, Bishop T.D. "Know Your Enemy." *YouTube Video.* Accessed August 25, 2017. https://www.youtube.com/watch?v=mxEBMVRcLrI.

McPartland, James C. and Ami Klin. "Asperger's syndrome." *Adolescent Medicine Clinics.* PMID 17030291. 2006.

Papisova, Vera. "Find Out When Most Teens Are Losing Their Virginity." *Teen Vogue,* September 30, 2015. http://www.teen-vogue.com/story/teens-losing-virginity-age.

Roemer, L., & Nagashima, K. (Directors), Muller, R. (Writer), & Rankin Jr, A., & Bass, J. (Producers). (1964). *Rudolph the Red-Nosed Reindeer*[Motion picture]. United States: Rankin Bass Productions.

Speaking Sound Doctrine Website. "Inappropriate Dancing." Accessed August 25, 2017. http://www.speakingsounddoctrine.com/Dancing.htm.

Thayer, Joseph Henry. A Greek–English Lexicon of the New

Testament. New York: Harper & Brothers. 1889. pp. 79-80.

The Stanton Peele Addiction Website. "I gave up everything for my boyfriend and now that he's left, I'm desolate." Accessed August 25, 2017. http://www.peele.net/faq/desolate.html.

ABOUT THE AUTHOR

Dane Fragger is married to his beautiful wife Asia Fragger. They are expecting their first child in April 2018.

Dane Fragger has 6 years of pastoral experience in youth and young adult ministry. God has given him an un-compromised message for young people across the nation.

For More information visit Dane at:

www.danefragger.com

If you've enjoyed this book,
we would love for you to do a review on Amazon.com

For prayer requests and book testimonies please email us:

youngandsaved@fraggerministries.com

Made in the USA
Columbia, SC
22 December 2019

85633678R00059